Unearthing

Common Sense

Through

Uncommon Quotes

(Picking the Minds of

Some Great and

Some not so Great

Individuals)

Generally, I am suspicious of quotes. I find that many people use them in an attempt to fabricate a false identity for themselves by hiding behind somebody else's famous coat. Usually, more weight is given to the celebrity status of the person quoted than to the content and the delivery of the extract, as if stardom by itself is an unmistakable authority on intelligence. Then, one night, while I was researching the properties of a particular herb, I came across a quote from Ralph Waldo Emerson that stated, "A weed is a plant, whose properties have not been discovered yet." I laughed and was astonished by the simplicity and the completeness of the definition. I put aside the health inquiry I was doing and suddenly I wanted to know more about this person. The more I read about him, the more amazed I became. I began searching for more quotes, hoping through them to find other interesting people I could relate to. The subjects were of a secondary importance. I believe that deeply thinking individuals can make any topic lively and enriching. On the other hand, even themes of palpitating interest cannot hide the deficiencies of a closed mind. For that reason, I didn't organize the book by subjects.

Sifting through the quotes, I encountered many familiar names like Napoleon, Aristotle, Churchill, Benjamin Franklin, etc. I've included their thoughts not because they are famous, but because they have said things worth thinking about. I also made some new surprisingly delightful acquaintances. For instance, I had never heard the name Robert Ingersoll before and I was astonished to learn that he is considered the greatest American speaker. I was shocked that such a great man had escaped my radar for so long. While I continued searching, the idea of collecting the quotes and assembling them into a book gradually took shape. I filtered through thousands of quotes, purging the ones with pathos, preaching, and political correctness and gathering only what I deem unadulterated common sense.

Pathos is like inflation. Both are counterfeiting tools for robbing people on a grand scale. I would rather listen to someone talking while sitting on the toilet dish, than to someone standing on a perch, brandishing fingers, and confounding pompousness with substance.

Preaching has more to do with establishing the controlling position of the preacher than with finding the true state of affairs. If I have to listen to a lecture, I prefer a tutor who is posing the right questions over one pretending to supply the "unassailable" truths, especially in areas where nothing can be proven.

Politically correct is an oxymoron. You are either political, glossing over subjects, or you are correct and shoot precisely.

Absurdity can be comical or tragic depending upon its distance from us. It is almost funny that the same institution, that was aggressively selling Indulgences for the absolution of every crime, is now a dispenser of moral norms and standards. The same organization, that burned scientists and books alike, is now posing as the light-bearer of society. I really don't know if I should be amused or scared by the scale and the frequency of insanities established as well-honored traditions. Paradoxes, in one form or another, rule our lives and that is why I also included sayings of people in prominent positions highlighting exactly that.

Jordan Lambev

ISBN-13: 978-1492903314

Duke of Wellington

All the business of war, and indeed all the business of life, is to endeavor to find out what you don't know by what you do; that's what I called 'guess what was at the other side of the hill'.

James J. Corbett

You become a champion by fighting one more round. When things are tough, you fight one more round.

Only those who have patience to do simple things perfectly ever acquire the skill to do difficult things easily.

Alex Haley

Anytime you see a turtle up on top of a fence post, you know he had some help.

Thomas Berger

No matter what side of the argument you are on, you always find people on your side that you wish were on the other.

Thomas Dekker

The calmest husbands make the stormiest wives.

Maxim Gorky

The most beautiful words in the English language are 'not guilty'.

When everything is easy one quickly gets stupid.

One has to be able to count if only so that at fifty one doesn't marry a girl of twenty.

Carl von Clausewitz

A conqueror is always a lover of peace.

Russell Hoban

Explorers have to be ready to die lost.

Wilt Chamberlain

Nobody roots for Goliath.

Chester W. Nimitz

A ship is always referred to as "she" because it costs so much to keep one in paint and powder.

3

Georg Wilhelm Friedrich Hegel

Genuine tragedies in the world are not conflicts between right and wrong. They are conflicts between two rights.

Scipio Africanus

I am convinced that life is 10% what happens to me and 96% how I react to it.

I'm never less at leisure than when at leisure, or less alone than when alone.

Faith Baldwin

Sometimes there is a greater lack of communication in facile talking than in silence.

Character builds slowly, but it can be torn down within incredible swiftness.

Charles Evans Hughes

When we lose the right to be different, we lose the privilege to be free.

Learned Hand

The spirit of liberty is the spirit which is not too sure that it is right.

Chinese proverbs

The best soldiers are not warlike.

A maker of IDOLS is never an idolater.

One never needs their humor as much as when they argue with a fool.

Govern a family as you would cook a small fish - very gently.

A truly great man never puts away the simplicity of a child.

A bad word whispered will echo a hundred miles.

Peter Drucker

The most important thing about communication is hearing what isn't said.

Most of what we call management consists of making it difficult for people to get their work done.

There is nothing so useless as doing efficiently that which should not be done at all.

Les Brown

Today you expand or you are expendable.

Stephen Covey

The only limits to the possibilities in your life tomorrow are the buts you use today.

Listen with the intent to understand, not with the intent to reply.

Imelda Marcos

I did not have three thousand pairs of shoes, I had one thousand and sixty.

Never dress down for the poor. They won't respect you for it. They want their First Lady to look like a million dollars.

If you know how much you've got, you probably haven't got much.

Filipinos want beauty. I have to look beautiful so that the poor Filipinos will have a star to look at from their slums.

If you know how rich you are, you are not rich. But me, I am not aware of the extent of my wealth. That's how rich we are.

We practically own everything in the Philippines.
It's the rich you can terrorize. The poor have nothing to lose.

My husband does not like me to give interviews because I say too much. No talk, no trouble.

They call me corrupt, frivolous. I am not at all privileged. Maybe the only privileged thing is my face. And corrupt? God! I would not look like this if I am corrupt. Some ugliness would settle down on my system.

Win or lose, we go shopping after the election.

Life is not a matter of place, things or comfort; rather, it concerns the basic human rights of family, country, justice and human dignity.

They went into my closets looking for skeletons, but thank God, all they found were shoes, beautiful shoes.

I hardly can sleep. I feel that my target now is really to save Mother Earth for humanity. And it's doable.

I really had no great love for shoes. I was a working First Lady; I was always in canvas shoes. I did nurture the shoes industry of the Philippines, and so every time there was a shoe fair, I would receive a pair of shoes as a token of gratitude.

Ferdinand was a gold trader. He was a lawyer for mining companies. When he entered politics in 1949, he had tons and tons of gold. When Bill Gates was a college dropout, Ferdinand already possessed billions of dollars and tons of gold. It wasn't stolen.

You know, not even your British Queen is called just Elizabeth - she's Elizabeth the Second. There's only one Imelda.

Leo Tolstoy

Truth, like gold, is to be obtained not by its growth, but by washing away from it all that is not gold.

William Gilmore Simms

I believe that economists put decimal points in their forecasts to show they have a sense of humor.

The dread of criticism is the death of genius.

Elbert Hubbard

He who does not understand your silence will probably not understand your words.

The teacher is the one who gets the most out of the lessons, and the true teacher is the learner.

Pray that success will not come any faster than you are able to endure it.

Creighton Abrams

When eating an elephant take one bite at a time.

If your library is not 'unsafe,' it probably isn't doing its job.

Viktor E. Frankl

Everything can be taken from a man but one thing: the last of human freedoms - to choose one's attitude in any given set of circumstances, to choose one's own way.

Between stimulus and response there is a space. In that space is our power to choose our response. In our response lies our growth and our freedom.

Dale Carnegie

Only the prepared speaker deserves to be confident.

Tim Heidecker

The idea that everyone's opinion is valuable is sometimes up for question.

It's never fun to read death threats.

Edward Teller

A fact is a simple statement that everyone believes. It is innocent, unless found guilty. A hypothesis is a novel suggestion that no one wants to believe. It is guilty, until found effective.

Life improves slowly and goes wrong fast, and only catastrophe is clearly visible.

Jean Rostand

Nothing is more admirable than the fortitude with which millionaires tolerate the disadvantages of their wealth.

It takes a very deep-rooted opinion to survive unexpressed.

Far too often the choices reality proposes are such as to take away one's taste for choosing.

We must watch over our modesty in the presence of those who cannot understand its grounds.

In politics, yesterday's lie is attacked only to flatter today's.

Mahatma Gandhi

First they ignore you, then they laugh at you, then they fight you, then you win.

There is more to life than increasing its speed.

Even if you are a minority of one, the truth is the truth.

When restraint and courtesy are added to strength, the latter becomes irresistible.

Konrad Adenauer

An infallible method of conciliating a tiger is to allow oneself to be devoured.

The art of politics consists in knowing precisely when it is necessary to hit an opponent slightly below the belt.

All parts of the human body get tired eventually - except the tongue.

The rare case where the conquered is very satisfied with the conqueror.

Lord Melbourne

Things are coming to a pretty pass when religion is allowed to invade private life.

Erwin Griswold

The right to be let alone is the underlying principle of the Constitution's Bill of Rights.

Michael Newdow

But in America, if you're an atheist, you lose.

I choose to worship not believing in God and government should not thrust a religious idea down my throat.

Those who deny the existence of a supreme being have been turned into second-class citizens by a government that continuously sends messages that 'real Americans' believe in God.

John Stuart Mill

There are many truths of which the full meaning cannot be realized until personal experience has brought it home.

Whatever crushes individuality is despotism, by whatever name it may be called and whether it professes to be enforcing the will of God or the injunctions of men.

The despotism of custom is everywhere the standing hindrance to human advancement.

Life has a certain flavor for those who have fought and risked all that the sheltered and protected can never experience.

The general tendency of things throughout the world is to render mediocrity the ascendant power among mankind.

James Anthony Froude

Science rests on reason and experiment, and can meet an opponent with calmness; but a belief is always sensitive.

Philosophy goes no further than probabilities, and in every assertion keeps a doubt in reserve.

Robert Green Ingersoll

Hope is the only universal liar who never loses his reputation for veracity.

The greatest test of courage on earth is to bear defeat without losing heart.

Ignorance is the soil in which belief in miracles grows.

It is an old habit with theologians to beat the living with the bones of the dead.

Reason, observation, and experience; the holy trinity of science.

There can be but little liberty on earth while men worship a tyrant in heaven.

Religion can never reform mankind because religion is slavery.

It is a thousand times better to have common sense without education than to have education without common sense.

If a man would follow, today, the teachings of the Old Testament, he would be a criminal. If he would follow strictly the teachings of the New, he would be insane.

I will not attack your doctrines nor your creeds if they accord liberty to me. If they hold thought to be dangerous - if they aver that doubt is a crime, then I attack them one and all, because they enslave the minds of men.

In nature there are neither rewards nor punishments; there are consequences.

The inspiration of the Bible depends upon the ignorance of the gentleman who reads it.

Poverty is not a virtue, nor is wealth a crime.

According to Christianity all that exist is an illusion and the only realities are things that don't exist.

Custom meets as at the cradle and leaves us at the tomb. Our first questions are answered by ignorance and our last by superstition.

I have little confidence in a business or any investment that promises dividends after the death of the stockholders.

Beyond the region of the Probable is the Possible and beyond the Possible is the Impossible and beyond the Impossible are the religions of the world.

Heresy is a cradle; orthodoxy a coffin.

They who demand hypocrisy must be satisfied with mediocrity.

A known infidel cannot get very rich, for the reason that the Christians are so forgiving and loving that they boycott him.

Every man who expresses an honest thought is a soldier in the army of the intellectual liberty.

A library is an arsenal.

After all man and a woman are the highest possible titles.

Salvation for credulity means damnation for investigation.

Ignorance has always been in the majority.

A few think; the many believe. The few lead; the many follow.

The best religion is common sense.

When the church had the absolute authority, then the world was the worst.

Man makes god in his own image and bad men are not apt to make a good god.

The supernatural is a mistake. I believe in the natural.

We have advanced just in the proportion that Christianity has lost power.

The human mind grows and as it grows it abandons the old, and the old gets its revenge by maligning the new.

Every good, ignorant, orthodox Christian places his bible above laws and constitutions. Every Christian believes god to be the source of all authority. I believe that authority to govern comes from the consent of the governed.

When science was a child religion sought to strangle it in the cradle.

Religion- a system by which this world is wasted in preparation for another.

The church is the enemy of human progress; it teaches every man to throw away his reason, to deny his observation and experience.

The stage thrusts the spear of ridicule through the shield of pretence.

Between the Catholics and the Protestants there has been about as much difference as there is between crocodiles and alligators.

Leo Rosten

First-rate people hire first-rate people; second-rate people hire third-rate people.

Some things are so unexpected that no one is prepared for them.

We see things as we are, not as they are.
Extremists think "communication" means agreeing with them.

I never cease being dumbfounded by the unbelievable things people believe.

Hermann Goering

Education is dangerous - every educated person is a future enemy.

Whenever I hear the word culture, I reach for my Browning!

Phyllis Bottome

To be in the right is often an expensive business.

Jack London

A bone to the dog is not charity. Charity is the bone shared with the dog, when you are just as hungry as the dog.

Diogenes

When I look upon seamen, men of science and philosophers, man is the wisest of all beings; when I look upon priests and prophets nothing is as contemptible as man.

It takes a wise man to discover a wise man.

The foundation of every state is the education of its youth.

It was a favorite expression of Theophrastus that time was the most valuable thing that a man could spend.

The art of being a slave is to rule one's master.

Galileo Galilei

We cannot teach people anything; we can only help them discover it within themselves.

All truths are easy to understand once they are discovered; the point is to discover them.

I have never met a man so ignorant that I couldn't learn something from him.

In questions of science, the authority of a thousand is not worth the humble reasoning of a single individual.

By denying scientific principles, one may maintain any paradox.

It vexes me when they would constrain science by the authority of the Scriptures, and yet do not consider themselves bound to answer reason and experiment.

I think that in the discussion of natural problems we ought to begin not with the Scriptures, but with experiments, and demonstrations.

And yet it moves.

It is surely harmful to souls to make it a heresy to believe what is proved.

Giordano Bruno

Time takes all and gives all.

Aesop

We hang the petty thieves and appoint the great ones to public office.

Men often applaud an imitation and hiss the real thing.

It is easy to be brave from a safe distance.

The smaller the mind the greater the conceit.

Our insignificance is often the cause of our safety.

The little reed, bending to the force of the wind, soon stood upright again when the storm had passed over. Plodding wins the race.

The level of our success is limited only by our imagination and no act of kindness, however small, is ever wasted.

After all is said and done, more is said than done. Example is the best precept.

The injuries we do and those we suffer are seldom weighed in the same scales.

Pericles

Just because you do not take an interest in politics doesn't mean politics won't take an interest in you. Freedom is the sure possession of those alone who have the courage to defend it.

Trees, though they are cut and loped, grow up again quickly, but if men are destroyed, it is not easy to get them again.

Henri Poincare

A very small cause which escapes our notice determines a considerable effect that we cannot fail to see, and then we say that the effect is due to chance.

Facts do not speak.

It is through science that we prove, but through intuition that we discover.

To invent is to discern, to choose. A small error in the former will produce an enormous error in the latter.

John Locke

No man's knowledge here can go beyond his experience.

New opinions are always suspected, and usually opposed, without any other reason but because they are not already common.

We are like chameleons, we take our hue and the color of our moral character, from those who are around us.

The only fence against the world is a thorough knowledge of it.

Reading furnishes the mind only with materials of knowledge; it is thinking that makes what we read ours.

The discipline of desire is the background of character.

Things of this world are in so constant a flux that nothing remains long in the same state.

It is easier for a tutor to command than to teach.

Ferdinand Foch

It takes 15,000 casualties to train a major general.

In whatever position you find yourself determine first your objective.

Baruch Spinoza

Do not weep; do not wax indignant. Understand.

All things excellent are as difficult as they are rare.

I have striven not to laugh at human actions, not to weep at them, nor to hate them, but to understand them.

The highest activity a human being can attain is learning for understanding, because to understand is to be free.

I call him free who is led solely by reason.

It may easily come to pass that a vain man may become proud and imagine himself pleasing to all when he is in reality a universal nuisance.

I have made a ceaseless effort not to ridicule, not to bewail, not to scorn human actions, but to understand them.

I do not know how to teach philosophy without becoming a disturber of established religion.

If you want the present to be different from the past, study the past.

I would warn you that I do not attribute to nature beauty or deformity, order or confusion. Only in relation to our imagination can things be called beautiful or ugly, well-ordered or confused.

None are more taken in by flattery than the proud, who wish to be the first and are not.

Men govern nothing with more difficulty than their tongues, and can moderate their desires more than their words.

Self-complacency is pleasure accompanied by the idea of oneself as cause.

The greatest pride, or the greatest despondency, is the greatest ignorance of one's self.

Whatsoever is contrary to nature is contrary to reason, and whatsoever is contrary to reason is absurd.

Fear cannot be without hope nor hope without fear.
To give aid to every poor man is far beyond the reach and power of every man. Care of the poor is incumbent on society as a whole.

Only that thing is free which exists by the necessities of its own nature, and is determined in its actions by itself alone.

Henry Brougham

Education makes a people easy to lead, but difficult to drive; easy to govern but impossible to enslave.

Harvey S. Firestone

Thought, not money is the real business capital.

John Wayne

Tomorrow is the most important thing in life. Comes into us at midnight very clean. It's perfect when it arrives and it puts itself in our hands. It hopes we've learned something from yesterday.

Life is tough, but it's tougher if you're stupid.

I suppose my best attribute, if you want to call it that, is sincerity. I can sell sincerity because that's the way I am.

Talk low, talk slow and don't say too much.

Oliver Wendell Holmes

A child's education should begin at least one hundred years before he is born.

Certitude is not the test of certainty. We have been cocksure of many things that were not so.

To have doubted one's own first principles is the mark of a civilized man.

The mind of a bigot is like the pupil of the eye. The more light you shine on it, the more it will contract.

The young man knows the rules, but the old man knows the exceptions.

Controversy equalizes fools and wise men in the same way - and the fools know it.

Nothing is so common-place as to wish to be remarkable.

It is the province of knowledge to speak, and it is the privilege of wisdom to listen.

Why can't somebody give us a list of things that everybody thinks and nobody says, and another list of things that everybody says and nobody thinks?

Do not be bullied out of your common sense by the specialist; two to one, he is a pedant.

Ray Bradbury

It's lack that gives us inspiration. It's not fullness.

Socrates

Employ your time in improving yourself by other men's writings, so that you shall gain easily what others have labored hard for.

Beware the barrenness of a busy life.

Be as you wish to seem.

Let him that would move the world first move himself.

Once made equal to man, woman becomes his superior.

Death may be the greatest of all human blessings.

Wisdom begins in wonder.

True wisdom comes to each of us when we realize how little we understand about life, ourselves, and the world around us.

Rudyard Kipling

A woman's guess is much more accurate than a man's certainty.

The silliest woman can manage a clever man; but it takes a very clever woman to manage a fool.

God could not be everywhere, and therefore he made mothers.

If history were taught in the form of stories, it would never be forgotten.

Leonardo da Vinci

Simplicity is the ultimate sophistication.

Learning never exhausts the mind.

The greatest deception men suffer is from their own opinions.

Life is pretty simple: You do some stuff. Most fails. Some works. You do more of what works. If it works big, others quickly copy it. Then you do something else. The trick is the doing something else.

I love those who can smile in trouble, who can gather strength from distress, and grow brave by reflection. 'Tis the business of little minds to shrink, but they whose heart is firm, and whose conscience approves their conduct, will pursue their principles unto death.

There are three classes of people: those who see, those who see when they are shown, those who do not see.

Art is never finished, only abandoned.

All our knowledge has its origins in our perceptions.

Water is the driving force of all nature.

He who loves practice without theory is like the sailor who boards ship without a rudder and compass and never knows where he may cast.

Iron rusts from disuse; water loses its purity from stagnation... even so does inaction sap the vigor of the mind.

The function of muscle is to pull and not to push, except in the case of the genitals and the tongue.

Just as courage imperils life, fear protects it.

As every divided kingdom falls, so every mind divided between many studies confounds and saps itself.

It's easier to resist at the beginning than at the end.

Nothing strengthens authority so much as silence.

The noblest pleasure is the joy of understanding.

I have been impressed with the urgency of doing. Knowing is not enough; we must apply. Being willing is not enough; we must do.

You can have no dominion greater or less than that over yourself.

Where there is shouting, there is no true knowledge.

Time stays long enough for anyone who will use it.

Medicine is the restoration of discordant elements; sickness is the discord of the elements infused into the living body.

He who wishes to be rich in a day will be hanged in a year.

You do ill if you praise, but worse if you censure, what you do not understand.

Necessity is the mistress and guide of nature. Necessity is the theme and inventress of nature, her curb and her eternal law.

Men of lofty genius when they are doing the least work are most active.

The natural desire of good men is knowledge.

The Medici created and destroyed me.

Although nature commences with reason and ends in experience it is necessary for us to do the opposite, that is to commence with experience and from this to proceed to investigate the reason.

Thomas Carlyle

No pressure, no diamonds.

Adversity is the diamond dust Heaven polishes its jewels with.

Endurance is patience concentrated.

When the oak is felled the whole forest echoes with it fall, but a hundred acorns are sown in silence by an unnoticed breeze.

Genius is an infinite capacity for taking pains.

No ghost was every seen by two pair of eyes.

Science must have originated in the feeling that something was wrong.

Every noble work is at first impossible.

Permanence, perseverance and persistence in spite of all obstacles, discouragements, and impossibilities: It is this, that in all things distinguishes the strong soul from the weak.

Nothing builds self-esteem and self-confidence like accomplishment.

There are good and bad times, but our mood changes more often than our fortune.

No great man lives in vain. The history of the world is but the biography of great men.

The block of granite which was an obstacle in the pathway of the weak, became a stepping-stone in the pathway of the strong.

What we become depends on what we read after all of the professors have finished with us. The greatest university of all is a collection of books.

Silence is the element in which great things fashion themselves together.

Weak eyes are fondest of glittering objects.

History shows that the majority of people that have done anything great have passed their youth in seclusion.

Originality is a thing we constantly clamour for, and constantly quarrel with.

If you do not wish a man to do a thing, you had better get him to talk about it; for the more men talk, the more likely they are to do nothing else.

A person who is gifted sees the essential point and leaves the rest as surplus.

The greatest of faults, I should say, is to be conscious of none.

I do not believe in the collective wisdom of individual ignorance.

Every new opinion, at its starting, is precisely in a minority of one.

It is a vain hope to make people happy by politics.

Xenophon

The sweetest of all sounds is praise.

The true test of a leader is whether his followers will adhere to his cause from their own volition, enduring the most arduous hardships without being forced to do so, and remaining steadfast in the moments of greatest peril.

Ralph Waldo Emerson

The first wealth is health.

Our chief want is someone who will inspire us to be what we know we could be.

This time, like all times, is a very good one, if we but know what to do with it.

Every mind must make its choice between truth and repose. It cannot have both.

The years teach much which the days never know.
As a cure for worrying, work is better than whiskey.
Every man I meet is in some way my superior.

Happy is the hearing man; unhappy the speaking man.

Nature and books belong to the eyes that see them.

Win as if you were used to it, lose as if you enjoyed it for a change.

Great men are they who see that spiritual is stronger than any material force - that thoughts rule the world.

People do not seem to realize that their opinion of the world is also a confession of character.

Once you make a decision, the universe conspires to make it happen.

There was never a child so lovely but his mother was glad to get him to sleep.

Every artist was first an amateur.

No change of circumstances can repair a defect of character.

A hero is no braver than an ordinary man, but he is brave five minutes longer.

The only way to have a friend is to be one.

A great man is always willing to be little.

Trust your instinct to the end, though you can render no reason.

Trust men and they will be true to you; treat them greatly and they will show themselves great.

Who you are speaks so loudly I can't hear what you're saying.

Bad times have a scientific value. These are occasions a good learner would not miss.

Shallow men believe in luck. Strong men believe in cause and effect.

A chief event of life is the day in which we have encountered a mind that startled us.

To be yourself in a world that is constantly trying to make you something else is the greatest accomplishment.

Love of beauty is taste. The creation of beauty is art.

Adopt the pace of nature: her secret is patience.

There is always safety in valor.

In every society some men are born to rule, and some to advise.

Manners require time, and nothing is more vulgar than haste.

The sum of wisdom is that time is never lost that is devoted to work.

The faith that stands on authority is not faith.

Why need I volumes, if one word suffice.
There is an optical illusion about every person we meet.

The value of a principle is the number of things it will explain.

The value of a dollar is social, as it is created by society.

If a man can... make a better mousetrap, the world will make a beaten path to his door.

Nothing astonishes men so much as common sense and plain dealing.

People that seem so glorious are all show; underneath they are like everyone else.

Fine manners need the support of fine manners in others.

Use what language you will, you can never say anything but what you are.

In skating over thin ice our safety is in our speed.

Some books leave us free and some books make us free.

Getting old is a fascination thing. The older you get, the older you want to get.

Our faith comes in moments; our vice is habitual.

We aim above the mark to hit the mark.

There are as many pillows of illusion as flakes in a snow-storm. We wake from one dream into another dream.

Every actual State is corrupt. Good men must not obey laws too well.

Pictures must not be too picturesque.

Fiction reveals truth that reality obscures.

One must be an inventor to read well. There is then creative reading as well as creative writing.

The creation of a thousand forests is in one acorn.

Science does not know its debt to imagination.

The invariable mark of wisdom is to see the miraculous in the common.

Every wall is a door.

The world is all gates, all opportunities, strings of tension waiting to be struck.

People with great gifts are easy to find, but symmetrical and balanced ones never.

Society is always taken by surprise at any new example of common sense.
Our greatest glory is not in never failing, but in rising up every time we fail.

What is a weed? A plant whose virtues have never been discovered.

Money often costs too much.

Before we acquire great power we must acquire wisdom to use it well.

We gain the strength of the temptation we resist.

People only see what they are prepared to see.

Make yourself necessary to somebody.

A great part of courage is the courage of having done the thing before.

As long as a man stands in his own way, everything seems to be in his way.

Charles Darwin

Ignorance more frequently begets confidence than does knowledge: it is those who know little, and not those who know much, who so positively assert that this or that problem will never be solved by science.

An American monkey, after getting drunk on brandy, would never touch it again, and thus is much wiser than most men.

In the long history of humankind (and animal kind, too) those who learned to collaborate and improvise most effectively have prevailed.

A scientific man ought to have no wishes, no affections, - a mere heart of stone.

If the misery of the poor be caused not by the laws of nature, but by our institutions, great is our sin.

I love fools' experiments. I am always making them.

To kill an error is as good a service as, and sometimes even better than, the establishing of a new truth or fact.

The mystery of the beginning of all things is insoluble by us; and I for one must be content to remain an agnostic.

Julius Caesar

It is better to create than to learn! Creating is the essence of life.

Experience is the teacher of all things.
As a rule, men worry more about what they can't see than about what they can.

No one is so brave that he is not disturbed by something unexpected.

If you must break the law, do it to seize power: in all other cases observe it.

It is not these well-fed long-haired men that I fear, but the pale and the hungry-looking.

Which death is preferably to every other? "The unexpected".

In war, events of importance are the result of trivial causes.

Oliver Cromwell

Keep your faith in God, but keep your powder dry.

Not only strike while the iron is hot, but make it hot by striking.

Do not trust the cheering, for those persons would shout as much if you or I were going to be hanged.

Necessity has no law.

We are Englishmen; that is one good fact.

Nature can do more than physicians.

Napoleon Bonaparte

Impossible is a word to be found only in the dictionary of fools.

A soldier will fight long and hard for a bit of colored ribbon.

Imagination rules the world.

Religion is what keeps the poor from murdering the rich.

Never interrupt your enemy when he is making a mistake.

A leader is a dealer in hope.

Never ascribe to malice that which is adequately explained by incompetence.

A celebrated people lose dignity upon a closer view.

If I had to choose a religion, the sun as the universal giver of life would be my god.

A revolution is an idea which has found its bayonets.

In politics stupidity is not a handicap.

I am sometimes a fox and sometimes a lion. The whole secret of government lies in knowing when to be the one or the other.
All religions have been made by men.

Soldiers generally win battles; generals get credit for them.

Power is my mistress. I have worked too hard at her conquest to allow anyone to take her away from me.

There are only two forces in the world, the sword and the spirit. In the long run the sword will always be conquered by the spirit.

A throne is only a bench covered with velvet.

Among those who dislike oppression are many who like to oppress.

Four hostile newspapers are more to be feared than a thousand bayonets.

Nothing is more difficult, and therefore more precious, than to be able to decide.

You must not fight too often with one enemy, or you will teach him all your art of war.

The people to fear are not those who disagree with you, but those who disagree with you and are too cowardly to let you know.

He who knows how to flatter also knows how to slander.

One must change one's tactics every ten years if one wishes to maintain one's superiority.

It requires more courage to suffer than to die.

It is the cause, not the death, which makes the martyr.

The act of policing is, in order to punish less often, to punish more severely.

Doctors will have more lives to answer for in the next world than even we generals.

Forethought we may have, undoubtedly, but not foresight.
Skepticism is a virtue in history as well as in philosophy.

There is one kind of robber whom the law does not strike at, and who steals what is most precious to men: time.

The truest wisdom is a resolute determination.

Victory belongs to the most persevering.

Men are more easily governed through their vices than through their virtues.

Men take only their needs into consideration - never their abilities.

Let the path be open to talent.

The human race is governed by its imagination.

Riches do not consist in the possession of treasures, but in the use made of them.

Take time to deliberate, but when the time for action has arrived, stop thinking and go in.

The battlefield is a scene of constant chaos. The winner will be the one who controls that chaos, both his own and the enemies.

I have only one counsel for you - be master.

I made all my generals out of mud.

We must laugh at man to avoid crying for him.

Religion is excellent stuff for keeping common people quiet.

In order to govern, the question is not to follow out a more or less valid theory but to build with whatever materials are at hand. The inevitable must be accepted and turned to advantage.

To do all that one is able to do, is to be a man; to do all that one would like to do, is to be a god.

There is only one step from the sublime to the ridiculous.

The first virtue in a soldier is endurance of fatigue; courage is only the second virtue.

The infectiousness of crime is like that of the plague.

The great proof of madness is the disproportion of one's designs to one's means.

The French complain of everything, and always.

Public opinion is the thermometer a monarch should constantly consult.

Respect the burden.

With audacity one can undertake anything, but not do everything.

One should never forbid what one lacks the power to prevent.

Ten people who speak make more noise than ten thousand who are silent.

The strong man is the one who is able to intercept at will the communication between the senses and the mind.

Henry Ford

If you think you can do a thing or think you can't do a thing, you're right.

It is well enough that people of the nation do not understand our banking and monetary system, for if they did, I believe there would be a revolution before tomorrow morning.

Coming together is a beginning; keeping together is progress; working together is success.

Anyone who stops learning is old, whether at twenty or eighty. Anyone who keeps learning stays young. The greatest thing in life is to keep your mind young.

Failure is simply the opportunity to begin again, this time more intelligently.

Thinking is the hardest work there is, which is probably the reason why so few engage in it.

There is one rule for the industrialist and that is: Make the best quality of goods possible at the lowest cost possible, paying the highest wages possible.

Even a mistake may turn out to be the one thing necessary to a worthwhile achievement.

If money is your hope for independence you will never have it. The only real security that a man will have in this world is a reserve of knowledge, experience, and ability.

I am looking for a lot of men who have an infinite capacity to not know what can't be done.

You can't build a reputation on what you are going to do.

My best friend is the one who brings out the best in me.

You can't learn in school what the world is going to do next year.

Nothing is particularly hard if you divide it into small jobs.

A market is never saturated with a good product, but it is very quickly saturated with a bad one.

Wealth, like happiness, is never attained when sought after directly. It comes as a by-product of providing a useful service.

I cannot discover that anyone knows enough to say definitely what is and what is not possible.

It has been my observation that most people get ahead during the time that others waste.

What's right about America is that although we have a mess of problems, we have great capacity - intellect and resources - to do some thing about them.

I do not believe a man can ever leave his business. He ought to think of it by day and dream of it by night.

Aristotle

We are what we repeatedly do. Excellence, then, is not an act, but a habit.

Anybody can become angry - that is easy, but to be angry with the right person and to the right degree and at the right time and for the right purpose, and in the right way - that is not within everybody's power and is not easy.

The worst form of inequality is to try to make unequal things equal.

Education is an ornament in prosperity and a refuge in adversity.

Pleasure in the job puts perfection in the work.

The aim of the wise is not to secure pleasure, but to avoid pain.

Bring your desires down to your present means. Increase them only when your increased means permit.

Youth is easily deceived because it is quick to hope.

Well begun is half done.

Probable impossibilities are to be preferred to improbable possibilities.

Men create gods after their own image, not only with regard to their form but with regard to their mode of life.

Friendship is essentially a partnership.

The young are permanently in a state resembling intoxication.

Dignity does not consist in possessing honors, but in deserving them.

The least initial deviation from the truth is multiplied later a thousand fold

Men acquire a particular quality by constantly acting in a particular way.

Bruce Lee

I fear not the man who has practiced 10,000 kicks once, but I fear the man who has practiced one kick 10,000 times.

A goal is not always meant to be reached, it often serves simply as something to aim at.

A wise man can learn more from a foolish question than a fool can learn from a wise answer.

If you always put limit on everything you do, physical or anything else. It will spread into your work and into your life. There are no limits. There are only plateaus, and you must not stay there, you must go beyond them.

A quick temper will make a fool of you soon enough.

As you think, so shall you become.

All fixed set patterns are incapable of adaptability or pliability. The truth is outside of all fixed patterns.

To hell with circumstances; I create opportunities.

To me, the extraordinary aspect of martial arts lies in its simplicity. The easy way is also the right way, and martial arts is nothing at all special; the closer to the true way of martial arts, the less wastage of expression there is.

Mike Tyson

It's good to know how to read, but it's dangerous to know how to read and not how to interpret what you're reading.

I'm not much for talking. You know what I do. I put guys in body bags when I'm right.

My biggest weakness is my sensitivity. I am too sensitive a person.

I was hoping he would get up so I could hit him again and keep him down.

Everybody's got plans... until they get hit.

I'm a dreamer. I have to dream and reach for the stars, and if I miss a star then I grab a handful of clouds.

George Washington

Guard against the impostures of pretended patriotism.

Over grown military establishments are under any form of government inauspicious to liberty, and are to be regarded as particularly hostile to republican liberty.

When we assumed the Soldier, we did not lay aside the Citizen.

Few men have virtue to withstand the highest bidder.

My observation is that whenever one person is found adequate to the discharge of a duty... it is worse executed by two persons, and scarcely done at all if three or more are employed therein.

It is far better to be alone, than to be in bad company.

Someday, following the example of the United States of America, there will be a United States of Europe.

Joseph Stalin

Education is a weapon whose effects depend on who holds it in his hands and at whom it is aimed.

The people who cast the votes don't decide an election, the people who count the votes do.

In the Soviet army it takes more courage to retreat than advance.

Print is the sharpest and the strongest weapon of our party.

Everyone imposes his own system as far as his army can reach.

Winston Churchill

A lie gets halfway around the world before the truth has a chance to get its pants on.

Continuous effort - not strength or intelligence - is the key to unlocking our potential.

Attitude is a little thing that makes a big difference.

A fanatic is one who can't change his mind and won't change the subject.

The best argument against democracy is a five-minute conversation with the average voter.

A politician needs the ability to foretell what is going to happen tomorrow, next week, next month, and next year. And to have the ability afterwards to explain why it didn't happen.

An appeaser is one who feeds a crocodile, hoping it will eat him last.

Success consists of going from failure to failure without loss of enthusiasm.

I am fond of pigs. Dogs look up to us. Cats look down on us. Pigs treat us as equals.

If we open a quarrel between past and present, we shall find that we have lost the future.

A prisoner of war is a man who tries to kill you and fails, and then asks you not to kill him.

Healthy citizens are the greatest asset any country can have.

I am easily satisfied with the very best.

I am an optimist. It does not seem too much use being anything else.

When you are winning a war almost everything that happens can be claimed to be right and wise.

Perhaps it is better to be irresponsible and right, than to be responsible and wrong.

There are two things that are more difficult than making an after-dinner speech: climbing a wall which is leaning toward you and kissing a girl who is leaning away from you.

Difficulties mastered are opportunities won.

The farther backward you can look, the farther forward you can see.

Play the game for more than you can afford to lose... only then will you learn the game.

There are a terrible lot of lies going about the world, and the worst of it is that half of them are true.

Nothing in life is so exhilarating as to be shot at without result.

Although prepared for martyrdom, I preferred that it be postponed.

Study history, study history. In history lie all the secrets of statecraft.

We are masters of the unsaid words, but slaves of those we let slip out.

Great and good are seldom the same man.

There is no such thing as public opinion. There is only published opinion.

I'm just preparing my impromptu remarks.

The first quality that is needed is audacity.

True genius resides in the capacity for evaluation of uncertain, hazardous, and conflicting information.
Sure I am of this, that you have only to endure to conquer.

The reserve of modern assertions is sometimes pushed to extremes, in which the fear of being contradicted leads the writer to strip himself of almost all sense and meaning.

I always avoid prophesying beforehand, because it is a much better policy to prophesy after the event has already taken place.

India is a geographical term. It is no more a united nation than the Equator.

The power of man has grown in every sphere, except over himself.

The problems of victory are more agreeable than those of defeat, but they are no less difficult.

War is mainly a catalogue of blunders.

The power of an air force is terrific when there is nothing to oppose it.

Mr. Attlee is a very modest man. Indeed he has a lot to be modest about.

It is more agreeable to have the power to give than to receive.

Muhammad Ali

I am the greatest, I said that even before I knew I was.

I hated every minute of training, but I said, 'Don't quit. Suffer now and live the rest of your life as a champion.

It's the repetition of affirmations that leads to belief. And once that belief becomes a deep conviction, things begin to happen.

A man who views the world the same at fifty as he did at twenty has wasted thirty years of his life.

He who is not courageous enough to take risks will accomplish nothing in life.

It's lack of faith that makes people afraid of meeting challenges, and I believed in myself.

The fight is won or lost far away from witnesses - behind the lines, in the gym, and out there on the road, long before I dance under those lights.

At home I am a nice guy: but I don't want the world to know. Humble people, I've found, don't get very far.

Only a man who knows what it is like to be defeated can reach down to the bottom of his soul and come up with the extra ounce of power it takes to win when the match is even.

The man who has no imagination has no wings.

It isn't the mountains ahead to climb that wear you out; it's the pebble in your shoe.

If they can make penicillin out of mouldy bread, they can sure make something out of you.

My way of joking is to tell the truth. That's the funniest joke in the world.

I figure I'll be champ for about ten years and then I'll let my brother take over - like the Kennedys down in Washington.

No one knows what to say in the loser's locker room.

Margaret Thatcher

Pennies do not come from heaven. They have to be earned here on earth.

Nothing is more obstinate than a fashionable consensus.

Being powerful is like being a lady. If you have to tell people you are, you aren't.

Albert Einstein

Insanity: doing the same thing over and over again and expecting different results.

A question that sometimes drives me hazy: am I or are the others crazy?

Any man who can drive safely while kissing a pretty girl is simply not giving the kiss the attention it deserves.

Only two things are infinite, the universe and human stupidity, and I'm not sure about the former.

It's not that I'm so smart, it's just that I stay with problems longer.

Great spirits have always encountered violent opposition from mediocre minds.

If you can't explain it simply, you don't understand it well enough.

Imagination is more important than knowledge.

A perfection of means, and confusion of aims, seems to be our main problem.

I have no special talent. I am only passionately curious.

Logic will get you from A to B. Imagination will take you everywhere.

If we knew what it was we were doing, it would not be called research, would it?

The only source of knowledge is experience.

Only one who devotes himself to a cause with his whole strength and soul can be a true master. For this reason mastery demands all of a person.

Intellectuals solve problems, geniuses prevent them.

Information is not knowledge.

Reality is merely an illusion, albeit a very persistent one.

The secret to creativity is knowing how to hide your sources.

As far as I'm concerned, I prefer silent vice to ostentatious virtue.

I think and think for months and years. Ninety-nine times, the conclusion is false. The hundredth time I am right.

Most people say that is it is the intellect which makes a great scientist. They are wrong: it is character.

The hardest thing to understand in the world is the income tax.

No amount of experimentation can ever prove me right; a single experiment can prove me wrong.

It is a miracle that curiosity survives formal education.

Science is a wonderful thing if one does not have to earn one's living at it.

Small is the number of people who see with their eyes and think with their minds.

You ask me if I keep a notebook to record my great ideas. I've only ever had one.

The important thing is not to stop questioning. Curiosity has its own reason for existing.

The environment is everything that isn't me.

We still do not know one thousandth of one percent of what nature has revealed to us.

People love chopping wood. In this activity one immediately sees results.

Sometimes one pays most for the things one gets for nothing.

When you are courting a nice girl an hour seems like a second. When you sit on a red-hot cinder a second seems like an hour. That's relativity.

The true sign of intelligence is not knowledge but imagination.

The difference between stupidity and genius is that genius has its limits.

We cannot solve our problems with the same thinking we used when we created them.

The only reason for time is so that everything doesn't happen at once.

Reality is merely an illusion, albeit a very persistent one. I have no special talent. I am only passionately curious. Few people are capable of expressing with equanimity opinions which differ from the prejudices of their social environment. Most people are even incapable of forming such opinions.

Once we accept our limits, we go beyond them.

Solitude is painful when one is young, but delightful when one is more mature.

Not everything that can be counted counts, and not everything that counts can be counted.

I am a deeply religious nonbeliever- this is a somewhat new kind of religion.

The monotony and solitude of a quiet life stimulates the creative mind.

Niels Bohr

Prediction is very difficult, especially if it's about the future.

An expert is a man who has made all the mistakes which can be made, in a narrow field.

Your theory is crazy, but it's not crazy enough to be true.

Every great and deep difficulty bears in itself its own solution. It forces us to change our thinking in order to find it.

The opposite of a fact is falsehood, but the opposite of one profound truth may very well be another profound truth.

Every sentence I utter must be understood not as an affirmation, but as a question.

How wonderful that we have met with a paradox. Now we have some hope of making progress.

Nikola Tesla

Today's scientists have substituted mathematics for experiments, and they wander off through equation after equation, and eventually build a structure which has no relation to reality.

I do not think you can name many great inventions that have been made by married men.

With ideas it is like with dizzy heights you climb: At first they cause you discomfort and you are anxious to get down, distrustful of your own powers; but soon the remoteness of the turmoil of life and the inspiring influence of the altitude calm your blood; your step gets firm and sure and you begin to look - for dizzier heights.

As in nature, all is ebb and tide, all is wave motion, so it seems that in all branches of industry, alternating currents - electric wave motion - will have the sway.

There is no memory or retentive faculty based on lasting impression. What we designate as memory is but increased responsiveness to repeated stimuli.

Erwin Rommel

Don't fight a battle if you don't gain anything by winning.

Otto von Bismarck

Laws are like sausages, it is better not to see them being made.

People never lie so much as after a hunt, during a war or before an election.

The main thing is to make history, not to write it.

When you want to fool the world, tell the truth.

With a gentleman I am always a gentleman and a half, and with a fraud I try to be a fraud and a half.

Never believe anything in politics until it has been officially denied.

There is a Providence that protects idiots, drunkards, children and the United States of America.

The preemptive war is like committing suicide for fear of death.

I have seen three emperors in their nakedness, and the sight was not inspiring.

Whoever speaks of Europe is wrong: it is a geographical expression.

The great questions of the day will not be settled by means of speeches and majority decisions but by iron and blood.

Be polite; write diplomatically; even in a declaration of war one observes the rules of politeness.

Charles Maurice the Talleyrand

Speech was given to man to disguise his thoughts.

Love of glory can only create a great hero; contempt of glory creates a great man.

Alexis de Tocqueville

The American Republic will endure until the day Congress discovers that it can bribe the public with the public's money.

In politics shared hatreds are almost always the basis of friendships.

Louis XIV –king of France

It is legal because I wish it.

Has God forgotten all I have done for Him.

Every time I appoint someone to a vacant position, I make a hundred unhappy and one ungrateful.

I am the state.

I could sooner reconcile all Europe than two women.

Catherine the Great

I praise loudly. I blame softly.

I shall be an autocrat, that's my trade; and the good Lord will forgive me, that's his.

If Russians knew how to read, they would write me off.

You philosophers are lucky men. You write on paper and paper is patient. Unfortunate Empress that I am, I write on the susceptible skins of living beings.

I may be kindly, I am ordinarily gentle, but in my line of business I am obliged to will terribly what I will at all.

I am one of the people who love the why of things.

The more a man knows, the more he forgives.

John Quincy Adams

Nip the shoots of arbitrary power in the bud, is the only maxim which can ever preserve the liberties of any people.

If your actions inspire others to dream more, learn more, do more and become more, you are a leader.

Posterity: you will never know how much it has cost my generation to preserve your freedom. I hope you will make good use of it.

A.J. Liebling

Freedom of the press is guaranteed only to those who own one.

The function of the press in society is to inform, but its role in society is to make money.

The way to write is well, and how is your own business.

Benjamin Franklin

We are all born ignorant, but one must work hard to remain stupid.

Guests, like fish, begin to smell after three days.

Tell me and I forget. Teach me and I remember. Involve me and I learn.

Life's Tragedy is that we get old to soon and wise too late.

Three can keep a secret, if two of them are dead.
Either write something worth reading or do something worth writing.

An investment in knowledge pays the best interest.

Remember not only to say the right thing in the right place, but far more difficult still, to leave unsaid the wrong thing at the tempting moment.

I wake up every morning at nine and grab for the morning paper. Then I look at the obituary page. If my name is not on it, I get up.

Who is wise? He that learns from everyone. Who is powerful? He that governs his passions. Who is rich? He that is content. Who is that? Nobody.

He that is good for making excuses is seldom good for anything else.

Do not fear mistakes. You will know failure. Continue to reach out.

He that would live in peace and at ease must not speak all he knows or all he sees.

Wise men don't need advice. Fools won't take it.

Take time for all things: great haste makes great waste.

Some people die at 25 and aren't buried until 75.

Energy and persistence conquer all things.

Even peace may be purchased at too high a price.

It takes many good deeds to build a good reputation, and only one bad one to lose it.

Whatever is begun in anger ends in shame.

Half a truth is often a great lie.

God helps those who help themselves.

It is only when the rich are sick that they fully feel the impotence of wealth.
Your net worth to the world is usually determined by what remains after your bad habits are subtracted from your good one.

If you would know the value of money, go and try to borrow some.

You may delay, but time will not.

Diligence is the mother of good luck.

Where liberty is, there is my country.

If a man empties his purse into his head, no one can take it from him.

The way to see by Faith is to shut the Eye of Reason.

When you're finished changing, you're finished.

Having been poor is no shame, but being ashamed of it, is.

He that speaks much, is much mistaken.
Creditors have better memories than debtors.

Tomorrow, every Fault is to be amended; but that tomorrow never comes.

Wars are not paid for in wartime, the bill comes later.

Observe all men, thyself most.

Remember that credit is money.

Leisure is the time for doing something useful. This leisure the diligent person will obtain the lazy one never.

The eye of the master will do more work than both his hands.

In the affairs of this world, men are saved not by faith, but by the want of it.

The worst wheel of the cart makes the most noise.

I saw few die of hunger; of eating, a hundred thousand.

Necessity never made a good bargain.
No nation was ever ruined by trade.

Democracy is a two wolfs and a lamb voting on what they are having for lunch. A Liberty is well armed lamb contesting the vote.

We are more heavily taxed by our idleness, pride and folly than we are taxed by the government.

He that won't be counseled won't be helped.

Success has ruined many a man.

Poverty often deprives a man of all spirit and virtue; it is hard for an empty bag to stand upright.

To find out a girl's faults, praise her to her girlfriends.

To be humble to superiors is duty, to equals courtesy, to inferiors nobleness.

The wise man draws more advantage from his enemies than the fool from his friends.

A learned blockhead is a greater blockhead than an ignorant one.

He that has a trade has an estate.

Nothing brings more pain than too much pleasure; nothing more bondage than too much liberty.

Wink at small faults; remember thou hast great ones.
Hear no ill of a friend, nor speak any of an enemy.

The busy man has few idle visitors; to the boiling pot the flies come not.

If you would reap praise you must sow the seeds, Gentle words and useful deeds.

Anger is never without a reason but seldom with a good one.

Love your neighbor yet don't pull down your hedge.

The heart of a fool is in his mouth, but the mouth of a wise man is in his heart.
Drink does not drown care, but waters it, and makes it grow fast.

Three good meals a day is bad living.

Here comes the orator! With his flood of words and his drop of reason.

He that lies down with dogs shall rise up with fleas.

Be slow in choosing a friend, slower in changing.

The sun never repents of the good he does, nor does he ever demand recompense.

Love your enemies for they tell you your faults.

Beware of little expenses, a small leak will sink a great ship.

Many have quarreled about religion that never practiced it.

Keep your eyes wide open before marriage, half shut afterwards.

None preaches better than the ant, and she says nothing.

He that composes himself is wiser than he that composes books.
What signifies knowing the names if you know not the natures of things?
In success be moderate.

Humility makes great men twice honorable.

When the well is dry – they know the worth of water.

There is much difference between imitating a good man and counterfeiting him.

As pride increases, fortune declines.

The things which hurt, instruct.

Would you persuade, speak of interest, not of reason.

In rivers and bad governments the lightest things swim at top.

The horse thinks one thing, and he that saddles him another.

Men and melons are hard to know.

It is better to take many injuries than to give one. An old young man will be a young old man.

Many dishes, many diseases.

Don't throw stones at your neighbors' if your own windows are glass.

Full of courtesy, full of craft.

He makes a Foe who makes a jest.

Wars bring scars.

Write Injuries in Dust, Benefits in Marble.

He that's secure is not safe.

Speak little, do much.

If you would be loved, love and be loveable.

Isaac Newton

Tact is the art of making a point without making an enemy.

Don Marquis

A pessimist is a person who has had to listen to too many optimists.

Middle age is the time when a man is always thinking that in a week or two he will feel as good as ever.

I have often noticed that ancestors never boast of the descendants who boast of ancestors. I would rather start a family than finish one. Blood will tell, but often it tells too much.

If you want to get rich from writing, write the sort of thing that's read by persons who move their lips when they're reading to themselves.

In order to influence a child, one must be careful not to be that child's parent or grandparent.

Successful people are the ones who think up things for the rest of the world to keep busy at.

An idea isn't responsible for the people who believe in it.

In all systems of theology the devil figures as a male person. Yes, it is women who keep the church going.

Bores bore each other too; but it never seems to teach them anything.

Man cannot be uplifted; he must be seduced into virtue.

There is luxury in self-reproach. When we blame ourselves, we feel no one else has a right to blame us.

Will Rogers

There are three kinds of men. The one that learns by reading. The few who learn by observation. The rest of them have to pee on the electric fence for themselves.

Alexander Hamilton started the U.S. Treasury with nothing, and that was the closest our country has ever been to being even.

Diplomacy is the art of saying "Nice doggie" until you can find a rock.

Good judgment comes from experience, and a lot of that comes from bad judgment.

About all I can say for the United States Senate is that it opens with a prayer and closes with an investigation.

Everything is changing. People are taking their comedians seriously and the politicians as a joke.

If you want to be successful, it's just this simple. Know what you are doing. Love what you are doing. And believe in what you are doing.

Ancient Rome declined because it had a Senate, now what's going to happen to us with both a House and a Senate?

I don't make jokes. I just watch the government and report the facts.

A man only learns in two ways, one by reading, and the other by association with smarter people.

Don't gamble; take all your savings and buy some good stock and hold it till it goes up, then sell it. If it don't go up, don't buy it.

I bet after seeing us, George Washington would sue us for calling him "father."

Everybody is ignorant, only on different subjects.

I'm not a real movie star. I've still got the same wife I started out with twenty-eight years ago.

Advertising is the art of convincing people to spend money they don't have for something they don't need.

This country has come to feel the same when Congress is in session as when the baby gets hold of a hammer.

The man with the best job in the country is the vice-president. All he has to do is get up every morning and say, "How is the president?"

People's minds are changed through observation and not through argument.

An ignorant person is one who doesn't know what you have just found out.

The worst thing that happens to you may be the best thing for you if you don't let it get the best of you.

A holding company is a thing where you hand an accomplice the goods while the policeman searches you.

The more you observe politics, the more you've got to admit that each party is worse than the other.

An onion can make people cry but there's never been a vegetable that can make people laugh.

If you ever injected truth into politics you have no politics.

There ought to be one day - just one - when there is open season on senators.

The fellow that can only see a week ahead is always the popular fellow, for he is looking with the crowd. But the one that can see years ahead, he has a telescope but he can't make anybody believe that he has it.

The income tax has made liars out of more Americans than golf.

People who fly into a rage always make a bad landing.

If the other fellow sells cheaper than you, it is called dumping. 'Course, if you sell cheaper than him, that's mass production.

Let advertisers spend the same amount of money improving their product that they do on advertising and they wouldn't have to advertise it.

Lettin' the cat outta the bag is a whole lot easier 'n puttin' it back in.

I read about eight newspapers in a day. When I'm in a town with only one newspaper, I read it eight times.

If you make any money, the government shoves you in the creek once a year with it in your pockets, and all that don't get wet you can keep.

The only way you can beat the lawyers is to die with nothing.

Money and women are the most sought after and the least known about of any two things we have.

When you put down the good things you ought to have done, and leave out the bad ones you did do well, that's Memoirs.

Make crime pay. Become a lawyer.

The farmer has to be an optimist or he wouldn't still be a farmer.

Things ain't what they used to be and never were.

Abraham Lincoln

America will never be destroyed from the outside. If we falter and lose our freedoms, it will be because we destroyed ourselves.

Always bear in mind that your own resolution to succeed is more important than any other.

Character is like a tree and reputation like a shadow. The shadow is what we think of it; the tree is the real thing.

Give me six hours to chop down a tree and I will spend the first four sharpening the axe.

This country, with its institutions, belongs to the people who inhabit it. Whenever they shall grow weary of the existing government, they can exercise their constitutional right of amending it, or exercise their revolutionary right to overthrow it.

Allow the president to invade a neighboring nation, whenever he shall deem it necessary to repel an invasion, and you allow him to do so whenever he may choose to say he deems it necessary for such a purpose - and you allow him to make war at pleasure.

I will prepare and some day my chance will come.

As I would not be a slave, so I would not be a master. This expresses my idea of democracy.

The philosophy of the school room in one generation will be the philosophy of government in the next.

The best thing about the future is that it comes one day at a time.

Books serve to show a man that those original thoughts of his aren't very new at all.

My great concern is not whether you have failed, but whether you are content with your failure.

It has been my experience that folks who have no vices have very few virtues.

No matter how much cats fight, there always seem to be plenty of kittens.

The best way to get a bad law repealed is to enforce it strictly.

Emperor Sigismund

I am the Roman Emperor, and am above grammar.

Edward Gibbon

I never make the mistake of arguing with people for whose opinions I have no respect.

Conversation enriches the understanding, but solitude is the school of genius.

A heart to resolve, a head to contrive, and a hand to execute.

The courage of a soldier is found to be the cheapest and most common quality of human nature.

Every man who rises above the common level has received two educations: the first from his teachers; the second, more personal and important, from himself.

Revenge is profitable, gratitude is expensive.

We improve ourselves by victories over ourselves. There must be contest, and we must win.

Style is the image of character.

Of the various forms of government which have prevailed in the world, an hereditary monarchy seems to present the fairest scope for ridicule.

The various modes of worship which prevailed in the Roman world were all considered by the people as equally true; by the philosopher as equally false; and by the magistrate as equally useful.

Our work is the presentation of our capabilities.

But the power of instruction is seldom of much efficacy, except in those happy dispositions where it is almost superfluous.

Walter Bagehot

The cure for admiring the House of Lords is to go and look at it.

An inability to stay quiet is one of the conspicuous failings of mankind.

Yogi Berra

You can observe a lot by just watching.

If you come to a fork in the road, take it.

It ain't over till it's over.

In theory there is no difference between theory and practice. In practice there is.

Always go to other people's funerals, otherwise they won't come to yours.

Half the lies they tell about me aren't true.
I never said most of the things I said.

Nobody goes there anymore. It's too crowded.

I wish I had an answer to that because I'm tired of answering that question.

The future ain't what it used to be.

There are some people who, if they don't already know, you can't tell 'em.

We made too many wrong mistakes.

It was impossible to get a conversation going, everybody was talking too much.

I usually take a two-hour nap from one to four.

Lord Chesterfield

Advice is seldom welcome, and those who need it the most, like it the least.

Be wiser than other people if you can, but do not tell them so.

Modesty is the only sure bait when you angle for praise.

Man cannot discover new oceans unless he has the courage to lose sight of the shore.
I sometimes give myself admirable advice, but I am incapable of taking it.

I recommend you to take care of the minutes, for the hours will take care of themselves.

The greatest art of a politician is to render vice serviceable to the cause of virtue.

I look upon indolence as a sort of suicide; for the man is effectually destroyed, though the appetites of the brute may survive.

A weak mind is like a microscope, which magnifies trifling things, but cannot receive great ones.

I find, by experience, that the mind and the body are more than married, for they are most intimately united; and when one suffers, the other sympathizes.

Judgment is not upon all occasions required, but discretion always is.

The less one has to do, the less time one finds to do it in.

Patience is the most necessary quality for business, many a man would rather you heard his story than grant his request.

Whoever is in a hurry shows that the thing he is about is too big for him.

Let them show me a cottage where there are not the same vices of which they accuse the courts.

He makes people pleased with him by making them first pleased with themselves.

Geoffrey Chaucer

The greatest scholars are not usually the wisest people.

The life so short, the crafts so long to learn.

Time and tide wait for no man.

Georges Clemenceau

All that I know I learned after I was thirty.

I don't know whether war is an interlude during peace, or peace an interlude during war.

A man's life is interesting primarily when he has failed - I well know. For it's a sign that he tried to surpass himself.

In order to act, you must be somewhat insane. A reasonably sensible man is satisfied with thinking.

It is far easier to make war than peace.

Al Capone

Capitalism is the legitimate racket of the ruling class.

Francis Ford Coppola

Usually, the stuff that's your best idea or work is going to be attacked the most.

You have to really be courageous about your instincts and your ideas. Otherwise you'll just knuckle under, and things that might have been memorable will be lost.

John Maynard Keynes

Education: the inculcation of the incomprehensible into the indifferent by the incompetent.

Successful investing is anticipating the anticipations of others.

The avoidance of taxes is the only intellectual pursuit that still carries any reward.

Americans are apt to be unduly interested in discovering what average opinion believes average opinion to be.

I work for a Government I despise for ends I think criminal.

Capitalism is the astounding belief that the most wickedest of men will do the most wickedest of things for the greatest good of everyone.

The difficulty lies not so much in developing new ideas as in escaping from old ones.

Ideas shape the course of history.

By a continuing process of inflation, government can confiscate, secretly and unobserved, an important part of the wealth of their citizens.

Words ought to be a little wild, for they are the assaults of thoughts on the unthinking.

Mao Zedong

In time of difficulties, we must not lose sight of our achievements.

Learn from the masses, and then teach them.

Frederick The Great

A crown is merely a hat that lets the rain in.

Religion is the idol of the mob; it adores everything it does not understand.

What is the good of experience if you do not reflect?

I begin by taking. I shall find scholars later to demonstrate my perfect right.

He who defends everything defends nothing.

The greatest and noblest pleasure which we have in this world is to discover new truths, and the next is to shake off old prejudices.

My people and I have come to an agreement which satisfied us both. They are to say what they please, and I am to do what I please.

If my soldiers were to begin to think, not one of them would remain in the army.

Niccolo Machiavelli

A prince never lacks legitimate reasons to break his promise.

Entrepreneurs are simply those who understand that there is little difference between obstacle and opportunity and are able to turn both to their advantage.

The more sand has escaped from the hourglass of our life, the clearer we should see through it.

He who wishes to be obeyed must know how to command.

The first method for estimating the intelligence of a ruler is to look at the men he has around him.

It is not titles that honor men, but men that honor titles.

The distinction between children and adults, while probably useful for some purposes, is at bottom a specious one, I feel. There are only individual egos, crazy for love.

Men rise from one ambition to another: first, they seek to secure themselves against attack, and then they attack others.

Where the willingness is great, the difficulties cannot be great.

Hence it comes about that all armed Prophets have been victorious, and all unarmed Prophets have been destroyed.

Princes and governments are far more dangerous than other elements within society.

Erich Maria Remarque

A hospital alone shows what war is.

Ralph Nader

Turn on to politics, or politics will turn on you.

Addiction should never be treated as a crime. It has to be treated as a health problem. We do not send alcoholics to jail in this country. Over 500,000 people are in our jails who are nonviolent drug users.

I once said to my father, when I was a boy, 'Dad we need a third political party.' He said to me, 'I'll settle for a second.'

Power has to be insecure to be responsive.

Clarence Darrow

I have never killed a man, but I have read many obituaries with great pleasure.

Chase after the truth like all hell and you'll free yourself, even though you never touch its coat tails.

The first half of our lives are ruined by our parents and the second half by our children.

I am an agnostic; I do not pretend to know what many ignorant men are sure of.

The world is made up for the most part of morons and natural tyrants, sure of themselves, strong in their own opinions, never doubting anything.

When I was a boy I was told that anybody could become President; I'm beginning to believe it.

The law does not pretend to punish everything that is dishonest. That would seriously interfere with business.

Depressions may bring people closer to the church but so do funerals.

To think is to differ.

I am a friend of the working man, and I would rather be his friend, than be one.

Just think of the tragedy of teaching children not to doubt.

Some of you say religion makes people happy. So does laughing gas.

Working people have a lot of bad habits, but the worst of these is work.

E. W. Howe

The way out of trouble is never as simple as the way in.

Never have children, only grandchildren.

Fifty percent of people won't vote, and fifty percent don't read newspapers. I hope it's the same fifty percent.

By the time a man gets to be presidential material, he's been bought ten times over.

Until the rise of American advertising, it never occurred to anyone anywhere in the world that the teenager was a captive in a hostile world of adults.

Democracy is supposed to give you the feeling of choice, like Painkiller X and Painkiller Y. But they're both just aspirin.

Our form of democracy is bribery, on the highest scale.

Today's public figures can no longer write their own speeches or books, and there is some evidence that they can't read them either.

Chuck Palahniuk

If you don't know what you want, you end up with a lot you don't.

Masochism is a valuable job skill.

When did the future switch from being a promise to a threat?

Peter De Vries

The value of marriage is not that adults produce children but that children produce adults.

Murals in restaurants are on a par with the food in museums.

When I can no longer bear to think of the victims of broken homes, I begin to think of the victims of intact ones.

John Updike

Writers may be disreputable, incorrigible, early to decay or late to bloom but they dare to go it alone.

Any activity becomes creative when the doer cares about doing it right or better.

By the time a partnership dissolves, it has dissolved.

Johann Wolfgang von Goethe

Dream no small dreams for they have no power to move the hearts of men.

None are more hopelessly enslaved than those who falsely believe they are free.

A person hears only what they understand.

Correction does much, but encouragement does more.

I love those who yearn for the impossible.

There are only two lasting bequests we can hope to give our children. One of these is roots, the other, wings.

Magic is believing in yourself, if you can do that, you can make anything happen.

A man's manners are a mirror in which he shows his portrait.

Love does not dominate; it cultivates.

We don't get to know people when they come to us; we must go to them to find out what they are like.

There is nothing so terrible as activity without insight.

It is not doing the thing we like to do, but liking the thing we have to do, that makes life blessed.

Nothing is more terrible than to see ignorance in action. Precaution is better than cure.

A clever man commits no minor blunders.

Be generous with kindly words, especially about those who are absent.

Go to foreign countries and you will get to know the good things one possesses at home.

Every step of life shows much caution is required.

A person places themselves on a level with the ones they praise.

Thomas Fuller

All things are difficult before they are easy.

Abused patience turns to fury.

If you command wisely, you'll be obeyed cheerfully.

A fool's paradise is a wise man's hell.

It is madness for sheep to talk peace with a wolf.

A conservative believes nothing should be done for the first time.

Many come to bring their clothes to church rather than themselves.

Travel makes a wise man better, and a fool worse.
Vows made in storms are forgotten in calm.

A lie has no leg, but a scandal has wings.

Compliments cost nothing, yet many pay dear for them.

In fair weather prepare for foul.

Two things a man should never be angry at: what he can help, and what he cannot help.

A good horse should be seldom spurred.

Care and diligence bring luck.

Don't let your will roar when your power only whispers.

Every horse thinks its own pack heaviest.

Learning hath gained most by those books by which the printers have lost.

Today is yesterday's pupil.

We ought to see far enough into a hypocrite to see even his sincerity.

All commend patience, but none can endure to suffer.

It is more difficult to praise rightly than to blame.

Men are more prone to revenge injuries than to requite kindness.

Pride will spit in pride's face.

If you are a master be sometimes blind , if you are servant, sometimes deaf.

Slight small injuries, and they will become none at all.

Change of weather is the discourse of fools.

Eaten bread is forgotten.
The patient is not likely to recover who makes the doctor his heir.

Not every question deserves an answer.

Antoine de Saint-Exupery

Perfection is achieved, not when there is nothing more to add, but when there is nothing left to take away.

Derek Bok

If you think education is expensive, try ignorance.

There is far too much law for those who can afford it and far too little for those who cannot.

Roy Cohn

I bring out the worst in my enemies and that's how I get them to defeat themselves.

William M. Evarts

The pious ones of Plymouth who, reaching the Rock, first fell upon their own knees and then upon the aborigines.

Louis Nizer

When a man points a finger at someone else, he should remember that four of his fingers are pointing at himself.

A man who works with his hands is a laborer; a man who works with his hands and his brain is a craftsman; but a man who works with his hands and his brain and his heart is an artist.

A graceful taunt is worth a thousand insults.

To find a fault is easy; to do better may be difficult.

Yes, there's such a thing as luck in trial law but it only comes at 3 o'clock in the morning. You'll still find me in the library looking for luck at 3 o'clock in the morning.

Fridtjof Nansen

The difficult is what takes a little time; the impossible is what takes a little longer.

Alas! Alas! Life is full of disappointments; as one reaches one ridge there is always another and a higher one beyond which blocks the view.

Friedrich Nietzsche

After coming into contact with a religious man I always feel I must wash my hands.

The best weapon against an enemy is another enemy.

In Christianity neither morality nor religion come into contact with reality at any point.

Those who cannot understand how to put their thoughts on ice should not enter into the heat of debate.

In individuals, insanity is rare; but in groups, parties, nations and epochs, it is the rule.

I cannot believe in a God who wants to be praised all the time.

We do not hate as long as we still attach a lesser value, but only when we attach an equal or a greater value.

Is man one of God's blunders? Or is God one of man's blunders?

F. Scott Fitzgerald

The test of a first-rate intelligence is the ability to hold two opposed ideas in mind at the same time and still retain the ability to function.

Show me a hero and I'll write you a tragedy.

Genius is the ability to put into effect what is on your mind.

Either you think, or else others have to think for you and take power from you, pervert and discipline your natural tastes, civilize and sterilize you.

Life is essentially a cheat and its conditions are those of defeat; the redeeming things are not happiness and pleasure, but the deeper satisfactions that come out of struggle.

Never confuse a single defeat with a final defeat.

You don't write because you want to say something, you write because you have something to say.

Often people display a curious respect for a man drunk, rather like the respect of simple races for the insane... There is something awe-inspiring in one who has lost all inhibitions.

Everybody's youth is a dream, a form of chemical madness.

To write it, it took three months; to conceive it three minutes; to collect the data in it all my life.

The victor belongs to the spoils.

Great art is the contempt of a great man for small art.
At eighteen our convictions are hills from which we look; at forty-five they are caves in which we hide.

Mark Twain

A person who won't read has no advantage over one who can't read.

A man who carries a cat by the tail learns something he can learn in no other way.

Kindness is the language which the deaf can hear and the blind can see.

Anger is an acid that can do more harm to the vessel in which it is stored than to anything on which it is poured.

I don't like to commit myself about heaven and hell - you see, I have friends in both places.

Don't let schooling interfere with your education.
All you need is ignorance and confidence and the success is sure.

Clothes make the man. Naked people have little or no influence on society.

The most interesting information comes from children, for they tell all they know and then stop.

I can live for two months on a good compliment.

Golf is a good walk spoiled.

It's not the size of the dog in the fight, it's the size of the fight in the dog.

What a wee little part of a person's life are his acts and his words! His real life is led in his head, and is known to none but himself.

Civilization is the limitless multiplication of unnecessary necessities.

I must have a prodigious quantity of mind; it takes me as much as a week sometimes to make it up.

Good breeding consists in concealing how much we think of ourselves and how little we think of the other person.

If man could be crossed with the cat, it would improve man but deteriorate the cat.

There is no sadder sight than a young pessimist.

Laws control the lesser man... Right conduct controls the greater one.

I was seldom able to see an opportunity until it had ceased to be one.

The difference between the right word and the almost right word is the difference between lightning and a lightning bug.

Familiarity breeds contempt - and children.

Only kings, presidents, editors, and people with tapeworms have the right to use the editorial "we."

The right word may be effective, but no word was ever as effective as a rightly timed pause.

It is better to deserve honors and not have them than to have them and not deserve them.

Necessity is the mother of taking chance.

Under certain circumstances, profanity provides a relief denied even to prayer.

Biographies are but the clothes and buttons of the man. The biography of the man himself cannot be written.

Noise proves nothing. Often a hen who has merely laid an egg cackles as if she laid an asteroid.

Never pick a fight with people who buy ink by the barrel.

Many a small thing has been made large by the right kind of advertising.

There are several good protections against temptation, but the surest is cowardice.

Truth is mighty and will prevail. There is nothing wrong with this, except that it ain't so.

Humor must not professedly teach and it must not professedly preach, but it must do both if it would live forever.

It usually takes me more than three weeks to prepare a good impromptu speech.

Martyrdom covers a multitude of sins.

Wit is the sudden marriage of ideas which before their union were not perceived to have any relation.

To refuse awards is another way of accepting them with more noise than is normal.

Prophesy is a good line of business, but it is full of risks.

It is easier to stay out than get out.

Get your facts first, then you can distort them as you please.

Forgiveness is the fragrance that the violet sheds on the heel that has crushed it.

You can't depend on your eyes when your imagination is out of focus.

Whenever you find yourself on the side of the majority, it is time to pause and reflect.

If it's your job to eat a frog, it's best to do it first thing in the morning. And If it's your job to eat two frogs, it's best to eat the biggest one first.

The best way to cheer yourself up is to try to cheer somebody else up.

Apparently there is nothing that cannot happen today.

The only way to keep your health is to eat what you don't want, drink what you don't like, and do what you'd rather not.

It's no wonder that truth is stranger than fiction. Fiction has to make sense.

The human race is a race of cowards; and I am not only marching in that procession but carrying a banner.

Thunder is good, thunder is impressive; but it is lightning that does the work.

It ain't those parts of the Bible that I can't understand that bother me, it is the parts that I do understand.

We have the best government that money can buy.

A person with a new idea is a crank until the idea succeeds.

It ain't what you don't know that gets you into trouble. It's what you know for sure that just ain't so.

Prosperity is the best protector of principle.

He is now rising from affluence to poverty.

The wit knows that his place is at the tail of a procession.

History shows that whenever a weak and ignorant people possess a thing which a strong and enlightened people want, it must be yielded up peaceably.

William Tecumseh Sherman

War is cruelty. There is no use trying to reform it. The crueler it is, the sooner it will be over.

In our Country... one class of men makes war and leaves another to fight it out.

He belonged to that army known as invincible in peace, invisible in war.

Bernice Fitz-Gibbon

Creativity varies inversely with the number of cooks involved in the broth.

Alexander Fleming

One sometimes finds what one is not looking for.

It is the lone worker who makes the first advance in a subject; the details may be worked out by a team, but the prime idea is due to enterprise, thought, and perception of an individual.

William Shakespeare

A fool thinks himself to be wise, but a wise man knows himself to be a fool.

It is not in the stars to hold our destiny but in ourselves.

When a father gives to his son, both laugh; when a son gives to his father, both cry.

It is a wise father that knows his own child.

Fishes live in the sea, as men do a-land; the great ones eat up the little ones.

Our doubts are traitors and make us lose the good we oft might win by fearing to attempt.

The course of true love never did run smooth.

Listen to many, speak to a few.

Pleasure and action make the hours seem short.
The empty vessel makes the loudest sound.

Reputation is an idle and most false imposition; oft got without merit, and lost without deserving.

The devil can cite Scripture for his purpose.

What is past is prologue.

To do a great right do a little wrong.

How sharper than a serpent's tooth it is to have a thankless child!

Maids want nothing but husbands, and when they have them, they want everything.

Some rise by sin, and some by virtue fall.

My pride fell with my fortunes.

Wisely, and slow. They stumble that run fast.

Sweet mercy is nobility's true badge.
Sweet are the uses of adversity which, like the toad, ugly and venomous, wears yet a precious jewel in his head.

145

Give your thoughts no tongue.

Come, gentlemen, I hope we shall drink down all unkindness.

The evil that men do lives after them; the good is oft interred with their bones.

I see that the fashion wears out more apparel than the man.

Time and the hour run through the roughest day.

When words are scarce they are seldom spent in vain.

Men shut their doors against a setting sun.

Ambition should be made of sterner stuff.

But men are men; the best sometimes forget.

John Heywood

Those who agree with us may not be right, but we admire their astuteness.

James A. Garfield

Ideas control the world.

Poverty is uncomfortable; but nine times out of ten the best thing that can happen to a young man is to be tossed overboard and compelled to sink or swim.

A pound of pluck is worth a ton of luck.

Next in importance to freedom and justice is popular education, without which neither freedom nor justice can be permanently maintained.

Franklin D. Roosevelt

Democracy cannot succeed unless those who express their choice are prepared to choose wisely. The real safeguard of democracy, therefore, is education.

The test of our progress is not whether we add more to the abundance of those who have much it is whether we provide enough for those who have little.

True individual freedom cannot exist without economic security and independence. People who are hungry and out of a job are the stuff of which dictatorships are made.

Here is my principle: Taxes shall be levied according to ability to pay. That is the only American principle.

Don't forget what I discovered that over ninety percent of all national deficits from 1921 to 1939 were caused by payments for past, present, and future wars.

Competition has been shown to be useful up to a certain point and no further, but cooperation, which is the thing we must strive for today, begins where competition leaves off.

The school is the last expenditure upon which America should be willing to economize.

Human kindness has never weakened the stamina or softened the fiber of a free people. A nation does not have to be cruel to be tough.

If I went to work in a factory the first thing I'd do is join a union.

The truth is found when men are free to pursue it.

David Lloyd George

Liberty is not merely a privilege to be conferred; it is a habit to be acquired.

The finest eloquence is that which gets things done.

Henry George

What has destroyed every previous civilization has been the tendency to the unequal distribution of wealth and power.

There is danger in reckless change, but greater danger in blind conservatism.

The man who gives me employment, which I must have or suffer, that man is my master, let me call him what I will.

Benjamin Disraeli

What we anticipate seldom occurs: but what we least expect generally happens.

Youth is a blunder; Manhood a struggle, Old Age a regret.

There is no education like adversity.

Seeing much, suffering much, and studying much, are the three pillars of learning.

Taking a new step, uttering a new word, is what people fear most.

Something unpleasant is coming when men are anxious to tell the truth.

How much easier it is to be critical than to be correct.

The secret of success is constancy to purpose.

Success is the child of audacity.

Beware of endeavoring to become a great man in a hurry. One such attempt in ten thousand may succeed. These are fearful odds.

Where knowledge ends, religion begins.

Desperation is sometimes as powerful an inspirer as genius.

Talk to a man about himself and he will listen for hours.

No man is regular in his attendance at the House of Commons until he is married.

My idea of an agreeable person is a person who agrees with me.

Next to knowing when to seize an opportunity, the most important thing in life is to know when to forego an advantage.

The palace is not safe when the cottage is not happy.

In politics nothing is contemptible.

As a general rule, the most successful man in life is the man who has the best information.

The fool wonders, the wise man asks.

Nine-tenths of the existing books are nonsense and the clever books are the refutation of that nonsense.

Upon the education of the people of this country the fate of this country depends.

Power has only one duty - to secure the social welfare of the People.

Mediocrity can talk, but it is for genius to observe.

Little things affect little minds.

Nobody is forgotten when it is convenient to remember him.

The more you are talked about the less powerful you are.

John Morley

You have not converted a man because you have silenced him.

No man can climb out beyond the limitations of his own character.

The great business of life is to be, to do, to do without and to depart.

Edward F. Halifax

Gratitude is one of those things that cannot be bought. It must be born with men, or else all the obligations in the world will not create it.

Those who are of the opinion that money will do everything may reasonably be expected to do everything for money.

Ignorance makes most men go into a political party, and shame keeps them from getting out of it.

Hope is generally a wrong guide, though it is very good company by the way.

A person may dwell so long upon a thought that it may take him a prisoner.

True merit, like a river, the deeper it is, the less noise it makes.

When people contend for their liberty they seldom get anything for their victory, but new masters.

John Lubbock

The important thing is not so much that every child should be taught, as that every child should be given the wish to learn.

A wise system of education will at last teach us how little man yet knows, how much he has still to learn.

Your character will be what you yourself choose to make it.

What we see depends mainly on what we look for.

B. H. Liddell Hart

A complacent satisfaction with present knowledge is the chief bar to the pursuit of knowledge.

The chief incalculable in war is the human will.

Loss of hope rather than loss of life is what decides the issues of war. But helplessness induces hopelessness.

In reality, it si more fruitful to wound than to kill. While the dead man lies still, counting only one man less, the wounded man is a progressive drain upon his side.

Lord Acton

And remember, where you have a concentration of power in a few hands, all too frequently men with the mentality of gangsters get control. History has proven that.

There are two things which cannot be attacked in front: ignorance and narrow-mindedness. They can only be shaken by the simple development of the contrary qualities. They will not bear discussion.

A wise person does at once, what a fool does at last. Both do the same thing; only at different times.

Learn as much by writing as by reading.

Be not content with the best book; seek sidelights from the others; have no favourites.

Arnold J. Toynbee

Civilizations die from suicide, not by murder.

Arthur Helps

Strength is born in the deep silence of long-suffering hearts; not amid joy.

We all admire the wisdom of people who come to us for advice.

Everywhere I have sought rest and not found it, except sitting in a corner by myself with a little book.

Having once decided to achieve a certain task, achieve it at all costs of tedium and distaste. The gain in self confidence of having accomplished a tiresome labor is immense.

Choose an author as you choose a friend.

Experience is the extract of suffering.

Oscar Wilde

A gentleman is one who never hurts anyone's feelings unintentionally.

Every saint has a past and every sinner has a future.

There are only two tragedies in life: one is not getting what one wants, and the other is getting it.
Experience is one thing you can't get for nothing.

As long as a woman can look ten years younger than her own daughter, she is perfectly satisfied.

If you pretend to be good, the world takes you very seriously. If you pretend to be bad, it doesn't. Such is the astounding stupidity of optimism.

I am not young enough to know everything.

A thing is not necessarily true because a man dies for it.

There are many things that we would throw away if we were not afraid that others might pick them up.

Woman begins by resisting a man's advances and ends by blocking his retreat.

Our ambition should be to rule ourselves, the true kingdom for each one of us; and true progress is to know more, and be more, and to do more.

Some cause happiness wherever they go; others whenever they go.

The truth is rarely pure and never simple.

Illusion is the first of all pleasures.

There is no sin except stupidity.

There is no necessity to separate the monarch from the mob; all authority is equally bad.

One should always play fairly when one has the winning cards.

Man can believe the impossible, but man can never believe the improbable.

The good ended happily, and the bad unhappily. That is what fiction means.

George Bernard Shaw

Life isn't about finding yourself. Life is about creating yourself.

Lee Iacocca

We are continually faced by great opportunities brilliantly disguised as insoluble problems.

The most successful businessman is the man who holds onto the old just as long as it is good, and grabs the new just as soon as it is better.

Miguel Indurain

To be free and to live a free life - that is the most beautiful thing there is.

Charles Kettering

Thinking is one thing no one has ever been able to tax.

An inventor fails 999 times, and if he succeeds once, he's in. He treats his failures simply as practice shots.

Problems are the price of progress. Don't bring me anything but trouble. Good news weakens me.

It doesn't matter if you try and try and try again, and fail. It does matter if you try and fail, and fail to try again.

The opportunities of man are limited only by his imagination. But so few have imagination that there are ten thousand fiddlers to one composer.

The world hates change, yet it is the only thing that has brought progress.

A problem well stated is a problem half-solved.

There will always be a frontier where there is an open mind and a willing hand.

The Wright brothers flew right through the smoke screen of impossibility.

The only time you mustn't fail is the last time you try.

Our imagination is the only limit to what we can hope to have in the future.

It is not a disgrace to fail. Failing is one of the greatest arts in the world.

There is a great difference between knowing and understanding: you can know a lot about something and not really understand it.

People think of the inventor as a screwball, but no one ever asks the inventor what he thinks of other people.

You can be sincere and still be stupid.

One fails forward toward success.

We often say that the biggest job we have is to teach a newly hired employee to fail intelligently... to experiment over and over again and to keep on trying and failing until he learns what will work.

Aldous Huxley

Dream in a pragmatic way.

Maybe this world is another planet's hell.

Facts do not cease to exist because they are ignored.

There is only one corner of the universe you can be certain of improving, and that's your own self.

That men do not learn very much from the lessons of history is the most important of all the lessons of history.

Experience teaches only the teachable.

An unexciting truth may be eclipsed by a thrilling lie.

All gods are homemade, and it is we who pull their strings, and so, give them the power to pull ours.

Most human beings have an almost infinite capacity for taking things for granted.

The secret of genius is to carry the spirit of the child into old age, which mean never losing your enthusiasm.

Experience is not what happens to you; it's what you do with what happens to you.

The more powerful and original a mind, the more it will incline towards the religion of solitude.

There isn't any formula or method. You learn to love by loving - by paying attention and doing what one thereby discovers has to be done.

Every man who knows how to read has it in his power to magnify himself, to multiply the ways in which he exists, to make his life full, significant and interesting.

I'm afraid of losing my obscurity. Genuineness only thrives in the dark.

Man approaches the unattainable truth through a succession of errors.

Orthodoxy is the diehard of the world of thought. It learns not, neither can it forget.

Thought must be divided against itself before it can come to any knowledge of itself.

Robert A. Heinlein

Don't handicap your children by making their lives easy.

Theology is never any help; it is searching in a dark cellar at midnight for a black cat that isn't there. Theologians can persuade themselves of anything.

Being right too soon is socially unacceptable.

Never insult anyone by accident.

Andrew Carnegie

People who are unable to motivate themselves must be content with mediocrity, no matter how impressive their other talents.

You cannot push anyone up the ladder unless he is willing to climb.

Concentrate your energies, your thoughts and your capital. The wise man puts all his eggs in one basket and watches the basket.

The average person puts only 25% of his energy and ability into his work. The world takes off its hat to those who put in more than 50% of their capacity, and stands on its head for those few and far between souls who devote 100%.

The men who have succeeded are men who have chosen one line and stuck to it.

J. Paul Getty

If you owe the bank $100 that's your problem. If you owe the bank $100 million, that's the bank's problem.

Jay Gould

I can hire one half of the working class to kill the other half.

Claude Levi-Strauss

The wise man doesn't give the right answers, he poses the right questions.

Arthur Schopenhauer

Talent hits a target no one else can hit; Genius hits a target no one else can see.

The wise have always said the same things, and fools, who are the majority have always done just the opposite.

All truth passes through three stages. First, it is ridiculed. Second, it is violently opposed. Third, it is accepted as being self-evident.

The doctor sees all the weakness of mankind; the lawyer all the wickedness, the theologian all the stupidity.

Every nation ridicules other nations, and all are right. Obstinacy is the result of the will forcing itself into the place of the intellect.

We forfeit three-quarters of ourselves in order to be like other people.

Just remember, once you're over the hill you begin to pick up speed.

Patriotism, when it wants to make itself felt in the domain of learning, is a dirty fellow who should be thrown out of doors.

The alchemists in their search for gold discovered many other things of greater value.

To live alone is the fate of all great souls.

The first forty years of life give us the text; the next thirty supply the commentary on it.

Great men are like eagles, and build their nest on some lofty solitude.

Every man takes the limits of his own field of vision for the limits of the world.

Treat a work of art like a prince. Let it speak to you first.

Religion is the masterpiece of the art of animal training, for it trains people as to how they shall think.

Politeness is to human nature what warmth is to wax.

Buying books would be a good thing if one could also buy the time to read them in: but as a rule the purchase of books is mistaken for the appropriation of their contents.

It is a clear gain to sacrifice pleasure in order to avoid pain.

Richard Nixon

When the President does it ,that means that it's not illegal.

I reject the cynical view that politics is a dirty business.

I'm glad I'm not Brezhnev. Being the Russian leader in the Kremlin. You never know if someone's tape recording what you say.

Voters quickly forget what a man says.

Dwight D. Eisenhower

If you want total security, go to prison. There you're fed, clothed, given medical care and so on. The only thing lacking... is freedom.

We will bankrupt ourselves in the vain search for absolute security.

I despise people who go to the gutter on either the right or the left and hurl rocks at those in the center.

Only Americans can hurt America.

We must guard against the acquisition of unwarranted influence, whether sought or unsought, by the military-industrial complex.

The purpose is clear. It is safety with solvency. The country is entitled to both.

Pessimism never won any battle.

Only strength can cooperate. Weakness can only beg.

The best morale exists when you never hear the word mentioned. When you hear a lot of talk about it, it's usually lousy.

James Madison

If Tyranny and Oppression come to this land, it will be in the guise of fighting a foreign enemy.

It is a universal truth that the loss of liberty at home is to be charged to the provisions against danger, real or pretended, from abroad.

In no instance have... the churches been guardians of the liberties of the people.

The advancement and diffusion of knowledge is the only guardian of true liberty.

Of all the enemies of public liberty, war is perhaps the most to be dreaded, because it comprises and develops the germ of every other.

Theodore Roosevelt

People ask the difference between a leader and a boss. The leader leads, and the boss drives.

Herbert Hoover

Blessed are the young for they shall inherit the national debt.

About the time we can make the ends meet, somebody moves the ends.

It is just as important that business keep out of government as that government keep out of business.

It is a paradox that every dictator has climbed to power on the ladder of free speech. Immediately on attaining power each dictator has suppressed all free speech except his own.

A good many things go around in the dark besides Santa Claus.

I'm the only person of distinction who has ever had a depression named for him.

Bertrand Russell

The trouble with the world is that the stupid are cocksure and the intelligent are full of doubt.

Advocates of capitalism are very apt to appeal to the sacred principles of liberty, which are embodied in one maxim: The fortunate must not be restrained in the exercise of tyranny over the unfortunate.

I would never die for my beliefs because I might be wrong.

The world is full of magical things patiently waiting for our wits to grow sharper.

I say quite deliberately that the Christian religion, as organized in its Churches, has been and still is the principal enemy of moral progress in the world.

A process which led from the amoeba to man appeared to the philosophers to be obviously a progress though whether the amoeba would agree with this opinion is not known.

Life is nothing but a competition to be the criminal rather than the victim.

Why is propaganda so much more successful when it stirs up hatred than when it tries to stir up friendly feeling?

I think we ought always to entertain our opinions with some measure of doubt. I shouldn't wish people dogmatically to believe any philosophy, not even mine.

The fundamental concept in social science is Power, in the same sense in which Energy is the fundamental concept in physics.

So far as I can remember, there is not one word in the Gospels in praise of intelligence.

The most savage controversies are about matters as to which there is no good evidence either way.
What is wanted is not the will to believe, but the will to find out, which is the exact opposite.

War does not determine who is right - only who is left.

The good life is one inspired by love and guided by knowledge.

Most people would sooner die than think; in fact, they do so.

One of the symptoms of an approaching nervous breakdown is the belief that one's work is terribly important.

In all affairs it's a healthy thing now and then to hang a question mark on the things you have long taken for granted.

There is something feeble and a little contemptible about a man who cannot face the perils of life without the help of comfortable myths.

The degree of one's emotions varies inversely with one's knowledge of the facts.

The secret to happiness is to face the fact that the world is horrible.

To teach how to live without certainty and yet without being paralysed by hesitation is perhaps the chief thing that philosophy, in our age, can do for those who study it.

A life without adventure is likely to be unsatisfying, but a life in which adventure is allowed to take whatever form it will is sure to be short.

Paul Samuelson

Politicians like to tell people what they want to hear - and what they want to hear is what won't happen.

Investing should be more like watching paint dry or watching grass grow. If you want excitement, take $800 and go to Las Vegas.

Good questions outrank easy answers.

George Steinbrenner

I will never have a heart attack. I give them.

Joshua Willis Alexander

There are many great truths which we do not deny, and which nevertheless we do not fully believe.

Tacitus

The more corrupt the state, the more numerous the laws.

Lao Tzu

Those who have knowledge, don't predict. Those who predict, don't have knowledge.

A leader is best when people barely know he exists, when his work is done, his aim fulfilled, they will say: we did it ourselves.

Kindness in words creates confidence. Kindness in thinking creates profoundness. Kindness in giving creates love.

A good traveler has no fixed plans, and is not intent on arriving.

Silence is a source of great strength.

Music in the soul can be heard by the universe.

From caring comes courage.

Anticipate the difficult by managing the easy.

He who knows, does not speak. He who speaks, does not know.

Respond intelligently even to unintelligent treatment.

Manifest plainness, embrace simplicity, reduce selfishness.

Charles V

Fortune has something of the nature of a woman. If she is too intensely wooed, she commonly goes the further away.

Voltaire

Common sense is not so common.

By appreciation, we make excellence in others our own property.

No snowflake in an avalanche ever feels responsible.
It is not enough to conquer; one must learn to seduce.

Clever tyrants are never punished.

One great use of words is to hide our thoughts.

It is one of the superstitions of the human mind to have imagined that virginity could be a virtue.

Nothing can be more contrary to religion and the clergy than reason and common sense.

The secret of being a bore... is to tell everything.

What most persons consider as virtue, after the age of 40 is simply a loss of energy.

Perfection is attained by slow degrees; it requires the hand of time.

Satire lies about literary men while they live and eulogy lies about them when they die.

The truths of religion are never so well understood as by those who have lost the power of reason.

The superfluous, a very necessary thing.

It is dangerous to be right in matters on which the established authorities are wrong.

Doubt is not a pleasant condition, but certainty is absurd.

Opinion has caused more trouble on this little earth than plagues or earthquakes.

Judge a man by his questions rather than his answers.

He must be very ignorant for he answers every question he is asked.

The true triumph of reason is that it enables us to get along with those who do not possess it.

We cannot always oblige; but we can always speak obligingly.

Louis-Ferdinand Celine

Experience is a dim lamp, which only lights the one who bears it.

Edmond de Goncourt

A painting in a museum hears more ridiculous opinions than anything else in the world.

If there is a God, atheism must seem to Him as less of an insult than religion.

Joseph Joubert

The aim of argument, or of discussion, should not be victory, but progress.

Ask the young. They know everything.

Genius begins great works; labor alone finishes them.

Those who never retract their opinions love themselves more than they love the truth.

William Arthur Ward

Adversity causes some men to break; others to break records.

The mediocre teacher tells. The good teacher explains. The superior teacher demonstrates. The great teacher inspires.

If you can imagine it, you can achieve it. If you can dream it, you can become it.

Happiness is an inside job.

Craig Washington

I prefer a man who will burn the flag and then wrap himself in the Constitution to a man who will burn the Constitution and then wrap himself in the flag.

185

Barbara Walters

Success can make you go one of two ways. It can make you a prima donna - or it can smooth the edges, take away the insecurities, and let the nice things come out.

James D. Watson

It's necessary to be slightly underemployed if you are to do something significant.

Thomas J. Watson

Recently, I was asked if I was going to fire an employee who made a mistake that cost the company $600,000. No, I replied, I just spent $600,000 training him. Why would I want somebody to hire his experience?

The way to succeed is to double your error rate.

A manager is an assistant to his men.

You will find success on the far side of failure.

Follow the path of the unsafe, independent thinker.

Woodrow Wilson

If you want to make enemies, try to change something.

When I give a man an office, I watch him carefully to see whether he is swelling or growing.

Prince Philip

When a man opens a car door for his wife, it's either a new car or a new wife.

Babe Ruth

Who is richer? The man who is seen, but cannot see? Or the man who is not being seen, but can see?

You just can't beat the person who never gives up.

Never let the fear of striking out get in your way.

Denis Diderot

Man will never be free until the last king is strangled with the entrails of the last priest.

From fanaticism to barbarism is only one step.

The philosopher has never killed any priests, whereas the priest has killed a great many philosophers.

Genius is present in every age, but the men carrying it within them remain benumbed unless extraordinary events occur to heat up and melt the mass so that it flows forth.

If there is one realm in which it is essential to be sublime, it is in wickedness. You spit on a petty thief, but you can't deny a kind of respect for the great criminal.

The God of the Christians is a father who makes much of his apples, and very little of his children.

There are things I can't force. I must adjust. There are times when the greatest change needed is a change of my viewpoint.

There is no good father who would want to resemble our Heavenly Father.

It is very important not to mistake hemlock for parsley, but to believe or not believe in God is not important at all.

Disturbances in society are never more fearful than when those who are stirring up the trouble can use the pretext of religion to mask their true designs.

The first step towards philosophy is incredulity.

We are far more liable to catch the vices than the virtues of our associates.

To attempt the destruction of our passions is the height of folly. What a noble aim is that of the zealot who tortures himself like a madman in order to desire nothing, love nothing, feel nothing, and who, if he succeeded, would end up a complete monster!

You have to make it happen.

Every man has his dignity. I'm willing to forget mine, but at my own discretion and not when someone else tells me to.

In order to shake a hypothesis, it is sometimes not necessary to do anything more than push it as far as it will go.

I drink to make other people interesting.

No advantages in this world are pure and unmixed.

Rene Descartes

Each problem that I solved became a rule, which served afterwards to solve other problems.

Common sense is the most fairly distributed thing in the world, for each one thinks he is so well-endowed with it that even those who are hardest to satisfy in all other matters are not in the habit of desiring more of it than they already have.

Divide each difficulty into as many parts as is feasible and necessary to resolve it.

You just keep pushing. You just keep pushing. I made every mistake that could be made. But I just kept pushing.

If you would be a real seeker after truth, it is necessary that at least once in your life you doubt, as far as possible, all things.

Except our own thoughts, there is nothing absolutely in our power.

Everything is self-evident.

The reading of all good books is like a conversation with the finest minds of past centuries.

I am indeed amazed when I consider how weak my mind is and how prone to error.

Benoit Mandelbrot

An extraordinary amount of arrogance is present in any claim of having been the first in inventing something.

A cloud is made of billows upon billows upon billows that look like clouds. As you come closer to a cloud you don't get something smooth, but irregularities at a smaller scale.

For much of my life there was no place where the things I wanted to investigate were of interest to anyone.

When the weather changes, nobody believes the laws of physics have changed. Similarly, I don't believe that when the stock market goes into terrible gyrations its rules have changed.

Desiderius Erasmus

When I get a little money I buy books; and if any is left I buy food and clothes.

Habit is overcome by habit.

He who allows oppression shares the crime.

Your library is your paradise.

Don't give your advice before you are called upon.

Human affairs are so obscure and various that nothing can be clearly known.

David Hume

Heaven and hell suppose two distinct species of men, the good and the bad. But the greatest part of mankind float between vice and virtue.

He is happy whom circumstances suit his temper; but he Is more excellent who suits his temper to any circumstance.

A wise man proportions his belief to the evidence.

And what is the greatest number? Number one.

Nothing is more surprising than the easiness with which the many are governed by the few.

A man acquainted with history may, in some respect, be said to have lived from the beginning of the world, and to have been making continual additions to his stock of knowledge in every century.

Human Nature is the only science of man; and yet has been hitherto the most neglected.

The heights of popularity and patriotism are still the beaten road to power and tyranny.

Scholastic learning and polemical divinity retarded the growth of all true knowledge.

It is not reason which is the guide of life, but custom.

Wernher von Braun

Research is what I'm doing when I don't know what I'm doing.

I have learned to use the word "impossible" with the greatest caution.

There is just one thing I can promise you about the outer-space program - your tax-dollar will go further.

Max Delbruck

Any living cell carries with it the experience of a billion years of experimentation by its ancestors.

Johannes Kepler

Nature uses as little as possible of anything.

Georg C. Lichtenberg

A book is a mirror: if an ape looks into it an apostle is hardly likely to look out.

Perhaps in time the so-called Dark Ages will be thought of as including our own.

Actual aristocracy cannot be abolished by any law: all the law can do is decree how it is to be imparted and who is to acquire it.

Doubt must be no more than vigilance, otherwise it can become dangerous.

He who says he hates every kind of flattery, and says it in earnest, certainly does not yet know every kind of flattery.

I am convinced we do not only love ourselves in others but hate ourselves in others too.

It is almost everywhere the case that soon after it is begotten the greater part of human wisdom is laid to rest in repositories.

Just as we outgrow a pair of trousers, we outgrow acquaintances, libraries, principles, etc., at times before they're worn out and times - and this is the worst of all - before we have new ones.

Many things about our bodies would not seem to us so filthy and obscene if we did not have the idea of nobility in our heads.

The human tendency to regard little things as important has produced very many great things.

There is no greater impediment to progress in the sciences than the desire to see it take place too quickly.

We have no words for speaking of wisdom to the stupid.
He who understands the wise is wise already.
Erudition can produce foliage without bearing fruit.

Nothing is more conducive to peace of mind than not having any opinion at all.

To do the opposite of something is also a form of imitation, namely an imitation of its opposite.

Robert Owen

You may depend upon it that they are as good hearts to serve men in palaces as in cottages.

William Cobbett

To be poor and independent is very nearly an impossibility.

You never know what you can do till you try.

Lord Salisbury

One of the nuisances of the ballot is that when the oracle has spoken you never know what it means.

Many who think they are workers in politics are really merely tools.

George Savile

He that leaveth nothing to chance will do few things ill, but he will do very few things.

A prince who will not undergo the difficulty of understanding must undergo the danger of trusting.

Our nature hardly allows us to have enough of anything without having too much.

Popularity is a crime from the moment it is sought; it is only a virtue where men have it whether they will or no.

The sight of a drunkard is a better sermon against that vice than the best that was ever preached on that subject.

The best way to suppose what may come, is to remember what is past.

Edward G. Bulwer-Lytton

A fool flatters himself, a wise man flatters the fool.

Anger ventilated often hurries towards forgiveness; anger concealed often hardens into revenge.

The best teacher is the one who suggests rather than dogmatizes, and inspires his listener with the wish to teach himself.

Genius does what it must, and talent does what it can.

A reform is a correction of abuses; a revolution is a transfer of power.

One of the surest evidences of friendship that one individual can display to another is telling him gently of a fault. If any other can excel it, it is listening to such a disclosure with gratitude, and amending the error.

There is nothing so agonizing to the fine skin of vanity as the application of a rough truth.

Every man who observes vigilantly and resolves steadfastly grows unconsciously into genius.

There is no such thing as luck. It's a fancy name for being always at our duty, and so sure to be ready when good time comes.

Herbert Spencer

Life is the continuous adjustment of internal relations to external relations.

A living thing is distinguished from a dead thing by the multiplicity of the changes at any moment taking place in it.

Divine right of kings means the divine right of anyone who can get uppermost.

Every cause produces more than one effect.

Our lives are universally shortened by our ignorance.

Society exists for the benefit of its members, not the members for the benefit of society.

Marriage: A word which should be pronounced 'mirage'.

Samuel Johnson

Your manuscript is both good and original; but the part that is good is not original, and the part that is original is not good.

Almost all absurdity of conduct arises from the imitation of those who we cannot resemble.

The greatest part of a writer's time is spent in reading in order to write. A man will turn over half a library to make a book.

Actions are visible, though motives are secret.

Margot Asquith

His modesty amounts to deformity.

Edward Cocker

Learn avidly. Question repeatedly what you have learned. Analyze it carefully. Then put what you have learned into practice intelligently.

John Galsworthy

Idealism increases in direct proportion to one's distance from the problem.

Horace Walpole

The wisest prophets make sure of the event first.

The whole secret of life is to be interested in one thing profoundly and in a thousand things well.

Jacques Pepin

After 45 years of marriage, when I have an argument with my wife, if we don't agree, we do what she wants. But, when we agree, we do what I want!

Philip Gibbs

It is better to give then to lend, and it costs about the same.

Katharine Whitehorn

The easiest way for your children to learn about money is for you not to have any.

Marlon Brando

Never confuse the size of your paycheck with the size of your talent.

Thomas Paine

All national institutions of churches, whether Jewish, Christian or Turkish, appear to me no other than human inventions, set up to terrify and enslave mankind, and monopolize power and profit.

Reason obeys itself; and ignorance submits to whatever is dictated to it.

Belief in a cruel God makes a cruel man.

One good schoolmaster is of more use than a hundred priests.

Persecution is not an original feature in any religion; but it is always the strongly marked feature of all religions established by law.

My mind is my own church.

That which we obtain too easily, we esteem too lightly.

War involves in its progress such a train of unforeseen circumstances that no human wisdom can calculate the end; it has but one thing certain, and that is to increase taxes.

Of all the tyrannies that affect mankind, tyranny in religion is the worst.

Titles are but nicknames, and every nickname is a title. When we are planning for posterity, we ought to remember that virtue is not hereditary.

Holbrook Jackson

Intuition is reason in a hurry.

No man is ever old enough to know better.

Your library is your portrait.

The time to read is any time: no apparatus, no appointment of time and place, is necessary. It is the only art which can be practiced at any hour of the day or night, whenever the time and inclination comes, that is your time for reading; in joy or sorrow, health or illness. A mother never realizes that her children are no longer children.

Roger Ascham

By experience we find out a short way by a long wandering.

It is costly wisdom that is bought by experience.

Learning teacheth more in one year than experience in twenty.

The least learned, for the most part, have been always most ready to write.

To speak as the common people do, to think as wise men do is style.

Joseph Addison

Three grand essentials to happiness in this life are something to do, something to love, and something to hope for.

An ostentatious man will rather relate a blunder or an absurdity he has committed, than be debarred from talking of his own dear person.

If you wish to succeed in life, make perseverance your bosom friend, experience your wise counselor, caution your elder brother, and hope your guardian genius.

Jesters do often prove prophets.

Men may change their climate, but they cannot change their nature. A man that goes out a fool cannot ride or sail himself into common sense.

Some virtues are only seen in affliction and others only in prosperity.

Talking with a friend is nothing else but thinking aloud.

Ernest Bramah

He who thinks he is raising a mound may only in reality be digging a pit.

Gerald Brenan

Wisdom is keeping a sense of fallibility of all our views and opinions.

You generally hear that what a man doesn't know doesn't hurt him, but in business what a man doesn't know does hurt.

Vera Brittain

I know one husband and wife who, whatever the official reasons given to the court for the break up of their marriage, were really divorced because the husband believed that nobody ought to read while he was talking and the wife that nobody ought to talk while she was reading.

Robert Burton

A dwarf standing on the shoulders of a giant may see farther than a giant himself.

Gilbert K. Chesterton

New roads; new ruts.

No man who worships education has got the best out of education... Without a gentle contempt for education no man's education is complete.

The simplification of anything is always sensational.

Some men never feel small, but these are the few men who are.

A yawn is a silent shout.

Agatha Christie

The secret of getting ahead is getting started.

Very few of us are what we seem.

The best time to plan a book is while you're doing the dishes.

Curious things, habits. People themselves never knew they had them.

Charles Caleb Colton

Much may be done in those little shreds and patches of time which every day produces, and which most men throw away.

None are so fond of secrets as those who do not mean to keep them.

If we steal thoughts from the moderns, it will be cried down as plagiarism; if from the ancients, it will be cried up as erudition.

To know a man, observe how he wins his object, rather than how he loses it; for when we fail, our pride supports us - when we succeed, it betrays us.

Constant success shows us but one side of the world; adversity brings out the reverse of the picture.

He that is good, will infallibly become better, and he that is bad, will as certainly become worse; for vice, virtue and time are three things that never stand still.

It is always safe to learn, even from our enemies; seldom safe to venture to instruct, even our friends.

No company is preferable to bad. We are more apt to catch the vices of others than virtues, as disease is far more contagious than health.

Our incomes should be like our shoes; if too small, they will gall and pinch us; but if too large, they will cause us to stumble and to trip.

That writer does the most who gives his reader the most knowledge and takes from him the least time.

The excess of our youth are checks written against our age and they are payable with interest thirty years later.

The first requisite for success is the ability to apply your physical and mental energies to one problem incessantly without growing weary.

There are three difficulties in authorship: to write anything worth publishing, to find honest men to publish it, and to find sensible men to read it.

The two most precious things this side of the grave are our reputation and our life. But it is to be lamented that the most contemptible whisper may deprive us of the one, and the weakest weapon of the other.

We ask advice, but we mean approbation.

It's no good running a pig farm badly for 30 years while saying, 'Really, I was meant to be a ballet dancer.' By then, pigs will be your style.

Fashion is what you adopt when you don't know who you are.

If at first you don't succeed, failure may be your style.

Abatement in the hostility of one's enemies must never be thought to signify they have been won over. It only means that one has ceased to constitute a threat.

You fall out of your mother's womb, you crawl across open country under fire, and drop into your grave.

The trouble with children is that they're not returnable.

John Harington

Treason doth never prosper, what's the reason? For if it prosper, none dare call it Treason.

Joseph McCabe

An idea or institution may arise for one reason and be maintained for quite a different reason.

Richard Whately

Lose an hour in the morning, and you will spend all day looking for it.

George Eliot

It is never too late to be what you might have been.

Adventure is not outside man; it is within.

Failure after long perseverance is much grander than never to have a striving good enough to be called a failure.

No story is the same to us after a lapse of time; or rather we who read it are no longer the same interpreters.

What do we live for, if not to make life less difficult for each other?

Knowledge slowly builds up what Ignorance in an hour pulls down.

The only failure one should fear, is not hugging to the purpose they see as best.

Vanity is as ill at ease under indifference as tenderness is under a love which it cannot return.

I like trying to get pregnant. I'm not so sure about childbirth.

One must be poor to know the luxury of giving!

Consequences are unpitying.

The finest language is mostly made up of simple unimposing words.

Susanna Moodie

Large parties given to very young children... foster the passions of vanity and envy, and produce a love of dress and display which is very repulsive in the character of a child.

Gelett Burgess

To appreciate nonsense requires a serious interest in life.

If in the last few years you haven't discarded a major opinion or acquired a new one, check your pulse. You may be dead.

Henry Ward Beecher

We should not judge people by their peak of excellence; but by the distance they have traveled from the point where they started.

The real man is one who always finds excuses for others, but never excuses himself.

Tears are often the telescope by which men see far into heaven.

A man's true state of power and riches is to be in himself. It is not the going out of port, but the coming in, that determines the success of a voyage.

Our best successes often come after our greatest disappointments.

The ability to convert ideas to things is the secret of outward success.

Books are not made for furniture, but there is nothing else that so beautifully furnishes a house.

The humblest individual exerts some influence, either for good or evil, upon others.

To become an able and successful man in any profession, three things are necessary, nature, study and practice.

You have come into a hard world. I know of only one easy place in it, and that is the grave.

He is greatest whose strength carries up the most hearts by the attraction of his own.
Of all escape mechanisms, death is the most efficient.

Archibald Alexander

Nature never makes any blunders, when she makes a fool she means it.

Norman Vincent Peale

Empty pockets never held anyone back. Only empty heads and empty hearts can do that.

Every problem has in it the seeds of its own solution. If you don't have any problems, you don't get any seeds.

It is of practical value to learn to like yourself. Since you must spend so much time with yourself you might as well get some satisfaction out of the relationship.

Stand up to your obstacles and do something about them. You will find that they haven't half the strength you think they have.

Be interesting, be enthusiastic... and don't talk too much.

The trouble with most of us is that we would rather be ruined by praise than saved by criticism.

The more you lose yourself in something bigger than yourself, the more energy you will have.

Part of the happiness of life consists not in fighting battles, but in avoiding them. A masterly retreat is in itself a victory.

Promises are like crying babies in a theater, they should be carried out at once.

We struggle with the complexities and avoid the simplicities.

Change yourself and your work will seem different.

You will soon break the bow if you keep it always stretched.

Understanding can overcome any situation, however mysterious or insurmountable it may appear to be.

Repetition of the same thought or physical action develops into a habit which, repeated frequently enough, becomes an automatic reflex.

Wilson Mizner

Don't talk about yourself; it will be done when you leave.

The most efficient water power in the world - women's tears.

I respect faith, but doubt is what gives you an education.

To profit from good advice requires more wisdom than to give it.

Do not be desirous of having things done quickly. Do not look at small advantages. Desire to have things done quickly prevents their being done thoroughly. Looking at small advantages prevents great affairs from being accomplished.

A good listener is not only popular everywhere, but after a while, he knows something.

If you steal from one author it's plagiarism; if you steal from many it's research.

In the battle of existence, Talent is the punch; Tact is the clever footwork.

A drama critic is a person who surprises the playwright by informing him what he meant.

Zora Neale Hurston

Those that don't got it, can't show it. Those that got it, can't hide it.

Gods always behave like the people who make them.

William Ralph Inge

Originality is undetected plagiarism.
Whoever marries the spirit of this age will find himself a widower in the next.

It is useless for the sheep to pass resolutions in favor of vegetarianism, while the wolf remains of a different opinion.

Alfred Nobel

I intend to leave after my death a large fund for the promotion of the peace idea, but I am skeptical as to its results.

Second to agriculture, humbug is the biggest industry of our age.

Alfred North Whitehead

The art of progress is to preserve order amid change and to preserve change amid order.

Familiar things happen, and mankind does not bother about them. It requires a very unusual mind to undertake the analysis of the obvious.

Not ignorance, but ignorance of ignorance, is the death of knowledge.

Fundamental progress has to do with the reinterpretation of basic ideas.

Andrew Wiles

However impenetrable it seems, if you don't try it, then you can never do it.

William Kingdon Clifford

We feel much happier and more secure when we think we know precisely what to do, no matter what happens, then when we have lost our way and do not know where to turn.

To know all about anything is to know how to deal with it under all circumstances.

Alan Turing

We can only see a short distance ahead, but we can see plenty there that needs to be done.

Ronald Fisher

In scientific subjects, the natural remedy for dogmatism has been found in research.

Pliny the Elder

The depth of darkness to which you can descend and still live is an exact measure of the height to which you can aspire to reach.

From the end spring new beginnings.

The best plan is to profit by the folly of others.

The only certainty is that nothing is certain.
No mortal man, moreover is wise at all moments.

Joseph Roux

When unhappy, one doubts everything; when happy, one doubts nothing.

There are people who laugh to show their fine teeth; and there are those who cry to show their good hearts.

Nothing vivifies, and nothing kills, like the emotions.

A fine quotation is a diamond in the hand of a man of wit and a pebble in the hand of a fool.

Solitude vivifies; isolation kills.

There is a slowness in affairs which ripens them, and a slowness which rots them.

The happiness which is lacking makes one think even the happiness one has unbearable.

Our experience is composed rather of illusions lost than of wisdom acquired.

Ernest Dimnet

Children have to be educated, but they have also to be left to educate themselves.

Most people suspend their judgment till somebody else has expressed his own and then they repeat it.

Henri de Lubac

Habit and routine have an unbelievable power to waste and destroy.

Cardinal De Retz

Nothing sways the stupid more than arguments they can't understand.

It is even more damaging for a minister to say foolish things than to do them.

Frank Lloyd Wright

The thing always happens that you really believe in; and the belief in a thing makes it happen.

Get the habit of analysis - analysis will in time enable synthesis to become your habit of mind.

Less is only more where more is no good.

There is nothing more uncommon than common sense.

E. F. Schumacher

Any intelligent fool can make things bigger and more complex... It takes a touch of genius - and a lot of courage to move in the opposite direction.

It might be said that it is the ideal of the employer to have production without employees and the ideal of the employee is to have income without work.

Many people love in themselves what they hate in others. Never let an inventor run a company. You can never get him to stop tinkering and bring something to market.

James Lovelock

An inefficient virus kills its host. A clever virus stays with it.

Sadly, it's much easier to create a desert than a forest.

Life does more than adapt to the Earth. It changes the Earth to its own purposes.

Douglas William Jerrold

Religion's in the heart, not in the knees.
The best thing I know between France and England is the sea.

In this world truth can wait; she is used to it.

The sharp employ the sharp.

John Ciardi

The day will happen whether or not you get up.

A good question is never answered. It is not a bolt to be tightened into place but a seed to be planted and to bear more seed toward the hope of greening the landscape of idea.

R. Buckminster Fuller

Don't fight forces, use them.

There is nothing in a caterpillar that tells you it's going to be a butterfly.

Love is metaphysical gravity.

How often I found where I should be going only by setting out for somewhere else.

Search others for their virtue, and yourself for your vices.

Most of my advances were by mistake. You uncover what is when you get rid of what isn't.

Tension is the great integrity.

If you are the master be sometimes blind, if you are the servant be sometimes deaf.

Edwin Land

An essential aspect of creativity is not being afraid to fail.

Marketing is what you do when your product is no good.

Don't undertake a project unless it is manifestly important and nearly impossible.

The most important thing about power is to make sure you don't have to use it.

Science is a method to keep yourself from kidding yourself.

J. R. R. Tolkien

Not all those who wander are lost.

Still round the corner there may wait, A new road or a secret gate.

Courage is found in unlikely places.

A box without hinges, key, or lid, yet golden treasure inside is hid.

All we have to decide is what to do with the time that is given us.

It's the job that's never started as takes longest to finish.

It does not do to leave a live dragon out of your calculations, if you live near him.

Short cuts make long delays.

Don't go getting mixed up in the business of your betters, or you'll land in trouble too big for you.

William Makepeace Thackeray

Next to excellence is the appreciation of it.

Bravery never goes out of fashion.

The two most engaging powers of an author are to make
new things familiar, familiar things new.

There are many sham diamonds in this life which pass
for real, and vice versa.
I would rather make my name than inherit it.

Meister Eckhart

Truly, it is in darkness that one finds the light, so when
we are in sorrow, then this light is nearest of all to us.

Stendhal

Only great minds can afford a simple style.

Groucho Marx

Alimony is like buying hay for a dead horse.

Dean Acheson

The manner in which one endures what must be endured is more important than the thing that must be endured.

The most important aspect of the relationship between the president and the secretary of state is that they both understand who is president.

Controversial proposals once soon become hallowed.

W. Edwards Deming

It is not enough to do your best; you must know what to do, and then do your best.

It is not necessary to change. Survival is not mandatory.

All anyone asks for is a chance to work with pride.

Rational behavior requires theory. Reactive behavior requires only reflex action.

Whenever there is fear, you will get wrong figures.

Any manager can do well in an expanding market.

Lack of knowledge... that is the problem.

I am forever learning and changing.

The big problems are where people don't realise they have one in the first place.

In 1945, the world was in a shambles. American companies had no competition. So nobody really thought much about quality. Why should they? The world bought everything America produced. It was a prescription for disaster.

Maxwell Maltz

Self-improvement is the name of the game, and your primary objective is to strengthen yourself, not to destroy an opponent.

Your most important sale in life is to sell yourself to yourself.

Our self image, strongly held, essentially determines what we become.

Take the trouble to stop and think of the other person's feelings, his viewpoints, his desires and needs. Think more of what the other fellow wants, and how he must feel.

To think, when one is no longer young, when one is not yet old, that one is no longer young, that one is not yet old, that is perhaps something.

Often the difference between a successful man and a failure is not one's better abilities or ideas, but the courage that one has to bet on his ideas, to take a calculated risk, and to act.

Isaac Asimov

The saddest aspect of life right now is that science gathers knowledge faster than society gathers wisdom.

People who think they know everything are a great annoyance to those of us who do.

Life is pleasant. Death is peaceful. It's the transition that's troublesome.

Never let your sense of morals get in the way of doing what's right.

A subtle thought that is in error may yet give rise to fruitful inquiry that can establish truths of great value.

Carl Sagan

Extinction is the rule. Survival is the exception.

Don't believe what your eyes are telling you. All they show is limitation. Look with your understanding, find out what you already know, and you'll see the way to fly.

Not being known doesn't stop the truth from being true.

Every problem has a gift for you in its hands.

Your friends will know you better in the first minute you meet than your acquaintances will know you in a thousand years.

Allow the world to live as it chooses, and allow yourself to live as you choose.

The simplest things are often the truest.

Ernest Hemingway

Never mistake motion for action.

The best way to find out if you can trust somebody is to trust them.

Courage is grace under pressure.

The world breaks everyone, and afterward, some are strong at the broken places.

We are all apprentices in a craft where no one ever becomes a master.

Once we have a war there is only one thing to do. It must be won. For defeat brings worse things than any that can ever happen in war.

Decadence is a difficult word to use since it has become little more than a term of abuse applied by critics to anything they do not yet understand or which seems to differ from their moral concepts.

As you get older it is harder to have heroes, but it is sort of necessary.

It's none of their business that you have to learn how to write. Let them think you were born that way.

The shortest answer is doing the thing.

When people talk, listen completely. Most people never listen.

There is no rule on how to write. Sometimes it comes easily and perfectly; sometimes it's like drilling rock and then blasting it out with charges.

All good books have one thing in common - they are truer than if they had really happened.

A man's got to take a lot of punishment to write a really funny book.

The world is a fine place and worth the fighting for and I hate very much to leave it.

All my life I've looked at words as though I were seeing them for the first time.

Wars are caused by undefended wealth.

Fear of death increases in exact proportion to increase in wealth.

Nathaniel Hawthorne

Easy reading is damn hard writing.

Richard Bausch

Every really good book was written a little at a time, over time, in tremendous confusion and doubt.

John Irving

If you are lucky enough to find a way of life you love, you have to find the courage to live it.

Good habits are worth being fanatical about.

Half my life is an act of revision.

You've got to get obsessed and stay obsessed.

Joseph Heller

Destiny is a good thing to accept when it's going your way. When it isn't, don't call it destiny; call it injustice, treachery, or simple bad luck.

The enemy is anybody who's going to get you killed, no matter which side he's on.

Jack Kerouac

I had nothing to offer anybody except my own confusion.

Great things are not accomplished by those who yield to trends and fads and popular opinion.

Norman Mailer

There is nothing safe about sex. There never will be.

There are four stages in a marriage. First there's the affair, then the marriage, then children and finally the fourth stage, without which you cannot know a woman, the divorce.

Once a newspaper touches a story, the facts are lost forever, even to the protagonists.

Every moment of one's existence one is growing into more or retreating into less. One is always living a little more or dying a little bit.

A modern democracy is a tyranny whose borders are undefined; one discovers how far one can go only by traveling in a straight line until one is stopped.

Growth, in some curious way, I suspect, depends on being always in motion just a little bit, one way or another.

Writing books is the closest men ever come to childbearing.

George Orwell

Freedom is the right to tell people what they do not want to hear.

Each generation imagines itself to be more intelligent than the one that went before it, and wiser than the one that comes after it.

All the war-propaganda, all the screaming and lies and hatred, comes invariably from people who are not fighting.

To survive it is often necessary to fight and to fight you have to dirty yourself.

Whoever is winning at the moment will always seem to be invincible.

Whatever is funny is subversive.

War against a foreign country only happens when the moneyed classes think they are going to profit from it.

In our time political speech and writing are largely the defense of the indefensible.

Myths which are believed in tend to become true.

The quickest way of ending a war is to lose it.

Saints should always be judged guilty until they are proved innocent.

Happiness can exist only in acceptance.

Political language... is designed to make lies sound truthful and murder respectable, and to give an appearance of solidity to pure wind.

Who controls the past controls the future. Who controls the present controls the past.

In a time of universal deceit - telling the truth is a revolutionary act.

Nationalism is power hunger tempered by self-deception. Liberal: a power worshipper without power.

James Allen

The law of harvest is to reap more than you sow. Sow an act, and you reap a habit. Sow a habit and you reap a character. Sow a character and you reap a destiny.

The more tranquil a man becomes, the greater is his success, his influence, his power for good. Calmness of mind is one of the beautiful jewels of wisdom.

Circumstances do not make the man, they reveal him.

You are today where your thoughts have brought you; you will be tomorrow where your thoughts take you.

You will become as small as your controlling desire; as great as you dominant aspiration.

The very fact that you are a complainer, shows that you deserve your lot.

A man is literally what he thinks.

In all human affairs there are efforts, and there are results, and the strength of the effort is the measure of the result.

When mental energy is allowed to follow the line of least resistance and to fall into easy channels, it is called weakness.

C. Benson

Very often a change of self is needed more than a change of scene.

George Borrow

Translation is at best an echo.

Two great talkers will not travel far together.

I am invariably of the politics of the people at whose table I sit, or beneath whose roof I sleep.

Leonard Woolf

Anyone can be a barbarian; it requires a terrible effort to remain a civilized man.

Georges Bernanos

Hope is a risk that must be run.

It's a fine thing to rise above pride, but you must have pride in order to do so.

Victor Hugo

Concision in style, precision in thought, decision in life.
Common sense is in spite of, not as the result of education.

Marcel Proust

Illness is the doctor to whom we pay most heed; to kindness, to knowledge, we make promise only; pain we obey.

The voyage of discovery is not in seeking new landscapes but in having new eyes.

We don't receive wisdom; we must discover it for ourselves after a journey that no one can take for us or spare us.

Like many intellectuals, he was incapable of saying a simple thing in a simple way.

We do not succeed in changing things according to our desire, but gradually our desire changes.

A fashionable milieu is one in which everybody's opinion is made up of the opinion of all the others. Has everybody a different opinion? Then it is a literary milieu.

What a profound significance small things assume when the woman we love conceals them from us.

All our final decisions are made in a state of mind that is not going to last.

Alexis Carrel

Man cannot remake himself without suffering, for he is both the marble and the sculptor.

Hard conditions of life are indispensable to bringing out the best in human personality.

In man, the things which are not measurable are more important than those which are measurable.

Life leaps like a geyser for those who drill through the rock of inertia.

Louis Pasteur

It is surmounting difficulties that makes heroes

Francois Jacob

Evolution is a tinkerer.

Ted Engstrom

Excellence is a process that should occupy all our days.

William Penn

Time is what we want most, but what we use worst.

Humility and knowledge in poor clothes excel pride and ignorance in costly attire.

Knowledge is the treasure of a wise man.

Sense shines with a double luster when it is set in humility. An able yet humble man is a jewel worth a kingdom.

True silence is the rest of the mind, and is to the spirit what sleep is to the body, nourishment and refreshment.

Alexander the Great

There is nothing impossible to him who will try.

I would rather excel others in the knowledge of what is excellent than in the extent of my powers and dominion.

Elizabeth I

All my possessions for a moment of time.

A fool too late bewares when all the peril is past.

Brass shines as fair to the ignorant as gold to the goldsmiths.

The stone often recoils on the head of the thrower.

King James I

I can make a lord, but only God can make a gentleman.

Marguerite de Valois

It is the same in love as in war; a fortress that parleys is half taken.

The more hidden the venom, the more dangerous it is.

Charlie Chaplin

Life is a tragedy when seen in close-up, but a comedy in long-shot.

To truly laugh, you must be able to take your pain, and play with it!

I suppose that's one of the ironies of life doing the wrong thing at the right moment.

John C. Maxwell

Most people want to avoid pain, and discipline is usually painful.

The experience of pain or loss can be a formidably motivating force.

Ideas have a short shelf life. You must act on them before the expiration date.

The greatest mistake we make is living in constant fear that we will make one.
Learn to say 'no' to the good so you can say 'yes' to the best.

Phillips Brooks

Character may be manifested in the great moments, but it is made in the small ones.

Do not pray for tasks equal to your powers. Pray for powers equal to your tasks.

Ostentation is the signal flag of hypocrisy.

J. K. Rowling

If you want to see the true measure of a man, watch how he treats his inferiors, not his equals.

Indifference and neglect often do much more damage than outright dislike.

Anything's possible if you've got enough nerve.

The truth. It is a beautiful and terrible thing, and must therefore be treated with great caution.

When people are very damaged, they can often meet the world with a kind of defiance.

The middle class is so funny, it's the class I know best, and it's the class where you find the most pretension, so that's what makes the middle classes so funny.

Failure means a stripping away of the inessential.

George Burns

Happiness is having a large, loving, caring, close-knit family in another city.

Acting is all about honesty. If you can fake that, you've got it made.

The secret of a good sermon is to have a good beginning and a good ending, then having the two as close together as possible.

Samuel Smiles

The very greatest things - great thoughts, discoveries, inventions - have usually been nurtured in hardship, often pondered over in sorrow, and at length established with difficulty.

Progress, of the best kind, is comparatively slow. Great results cannot be achieved at once; and we must be satisfied to advance in life as we walk, step by step.

We often discover what will do, by finding out what will not do; and probably he who never made a mistake never made a discovery.

The shortest way to do many things is to do only one thing at once.

The apprenticeship of difficulty is one which the greatest of men have had to serve.

Roy Hattersley

Familiarity with evil breeds not contempt but acceptance.

Alexander Graham Bell

The most successful men in the end are those whose success is the result of steady accretion.

America is a country of inventors, and the greatest of inventors are the newspaper men.

Johann Heinrich Lambert

I understood that the will could not be improved before the mind had been enlightened.

Pythagoras

The oldest, shortest words - 'yes' and 'no' - are those which require the most thought.

Strength of mind rests in sobriety; for this keeps your reason unclouded by passion.

Adam Smith

The real tragedy of the poor is the poverty of their aspirations.

All money is a matter of belief.

Labour was the first price, the original purchase - money that was paid for all things. It was not by gold or by silver, but by labour, that all wealth of the world was originally purchased.

Virtue is more to be feared than vice, because its excesses are not subject to the regulation of conscience.

Happiness never lays its finger on its pulse.

No complaint... is more common than that of a scarcity of money.

Adventure upon all the tickets in the lottery, and you lose for certain; and the greater the number of your tickets the nearer your approach to this certainty.

Science is the great antidote to the poison of enthusiasm and superstition.

As soon as the land of any country has all become private property, the landlords, like all other men, love to reap where they never sowed, and demand a rent even for its natural produce.

Walter Scott

All men who have turned out worth anything have had the chief hand in their own education.

He is the best sailor who can steer within fewest points of the wind, and exact a motive power out of the greatest obstacles.

A rusty nail placed near a faithful compass, will sway it from the truth, and wreck the argosy.

Friedrich August von Hayek

The curious task of economics is to demonstrate to men how little they really know about what they imagine they can design.

We shall not grow wiser before we learn that much that we have done was very foolish.

'Emergencies' have always been the pretext on which the safeguards of individual liberty have been eroded.

Quintus Tullius Cicero

During war, the laws are silent.

Avoid any specific discussion of public policy at public meetings.

Carl Jung

We cannot change anything until we accept it. Condemnation does not liberate, it oppresses.

The shoe that fits one person pinches another; there is no recipe for living that suits all cases.

The meeting of two personalities is like the contact of two chemical substances: if there is any reaction, both are transformed.

Everything that irritates us about others can lead us to an understanding of ourselves.

Knowledge rests not upon truth alone, but upon error also.

The wine of youth does not always clear with advancing years; sometimes it grows turbid.

Man needs difficulties; they are necessary for health.

Bertolt Brecht

It is easier to rob by setting up a bank than by holding up a bank clerk.

Hungry man, reach for the book: it is a weapon.

The defeats and victories of the fellows at the top aren't always defeats and victories for the fellows at the bottom.

He who laughs has not yet heard the bad news.

There are many elements to a campaign. Leadership is number one. Everything else is number two.
War is like love; it always finds a way.

Science knows only one commandment - contribute to science.

Heinrich Heine

The Wedding March always reminds me of the music played when soldiers go into battle.

Experience is a good school. But the fees are high.

Talking and eloquence are not the same: to speak and to speak well are two things.

True eloquence consists in saying all that is necessary, and nothing but what is necessary.

When the heroes go off the stage, the clowns come on.

The men of action are, after all, only the unconscious instruments of the men of thought.

James Buchanan

What is right and what is practicable are two different things.

The test of leadership is not to put greatness into humanity, but to elicit it, for the greatness is already there.

Kaiser Wilhelm II

Give me a woman who loves beer and I will conquer the world.